DIRT CHEAP VALUABLE
SURVIVAL
RETREAT

Facts You Never Knew About

Getting An Inexpensive,

Off-Grid, Defensible,

SHTF Survival Retreat

By Cal Wilson

Dirt Cheap Valuable Survival Retreat
Facts You Never Knew About Getting An Inexpensive, Off Grid, Defendable,
SHTF Survival Retreat

ISBN-10: 1546860665
ISBN-13: 978-1546860662

Table Of Contents

Introduction

We Americans are a pretty unprepared bunch.

A 2015 Federal Emergency Management Agency (FEMA) survey found that in the previous year, nearly 60 percent of Americans have not practiced a disaster drill or preparedness exercise at work, school, or home. Further, only 39 percent of Americans had developed any emergency plan or even discussed one with their household.

"Well," you might say, "those are the Americans who must live away from where all the disasters happen. That figures."

Not so! FEMA went on to report that 80 percent of Americans live in counties that have been hit by weather-related disasters since 2007, so they have no excuse.

Lack of stored food is another problem. A 2012 survey by CBN revealed that over half of Americans have less than a three-day supply of food on hand. It seems that Americans wait for disasters, and *then* begin planning for them – just the opposite of how it should be done.

It gets even worse with personal financial preparedness. A recent Corporation for Enterprise Development survey found that after paying the extra expenses due to a lost job or needing an unexpected medical procedure, nearly 44 percent of American households would not even have enough money to cover their basic living expenses.

That's a lot of Americans who are barely hanging on. Since 2005, our country has experienced some horrible hurricanes, tornados, floods and wildfires, even an Ebola scare in 2014 that could have become a major pandemic. Many people still don't know that in July 2012, the Earth nearly missed a solar superstorm, known as a coronal mass ejection (CME), which could have fried electronics and crippled most of our national infrastructure. Don't believe me? Look it up: NASA reported on it, in an article entitled "Near Miss: The Solar Superstorm of July 2012."

Good thing that in a recent National Geographic survey, 76% of Americans would be willing to share their resources or supplies in time of disaster. But come to think of it, most Americans have little or no stored food to share anyway, so it doesn't matter!

Let's face it: we live in a dangerous world, and most of the country is woefully unprepared for the next big disaster. And a major disaster is not that far-fetched. If that CME in 2012 had happened nine days earlier and had hit the Earth, do you really think we would just stay in the dark for a few months and then unite in a recovery? There are specialists who were quoted in articles about that event, and I'm pretty sure they weren't kidding. Call me skeptical, but I just don't buy it.

The reality of a 2012 CME that almost happened, or in the Ebola pandemic that could have happened in 2014, or with any other national catastrophe on the horizon is this: there would be a major disruption in food, water, power, and eventually the rule of law. Those city-dwellers who were smart enough to stock up on food and water would have survived for a while, but looting and government-inspired rationing of whatever is left would probably become the order of the day.

And once the food in the cities is all gone, the hungry survivors will go outside of town and loot the places that have food there. Many family-operated farms and ranches will be overrun, and all the food taken. Only the rare survival retreats that are hidden, and prepared with a retreat group, would survive.

If you think getting such a survival retreat is out of your reach, think again. In the pages that follow, I will detail how to get a retreat that is inexpensive, powered off-grid and defensible: a survival retreat that will greatly enhance the odds of you and your family surviving a future SHTF event. I will speak not only from my experience from having bought my own survival retreat, but I will also present testimonials from others who have gone through many of the issues discussed here.

Here's another thing: while I am thrilled that I now have in place my family's honest-to-goodness survival retreat, the tone of this book might at times sound negative. Please do not take that to mean that it is frustrating or difficult to have such a property. It's not. While it can be a challenge at times, it is a real delight to have a large piece of land out in the country where my family and friends can survive in a time of disaster. But I have learned a lot of lessons about my survival retreat the hard way, and I now wish to pass along to you those lessons. So please don't be discouraged from the warnings in this book. They are included here to teach.

In fact, instead of being discouraged, I encourage you to be confident with the issues presented here. In prepping, as in life, you are best served by a can-do attitude, one that views any setbacks as temporary, merely a short delay in a goal that you will someday achieve. And, despite the fact that you may be venturing into a territory that is totally uncharted for you – buying a large piece on property in the country -- do not be intimidated. Many people before you have done this, and there is no reason why you cannot do it too.

At the same time, I would like to include a brief comment on following laws. In no way is the content of this book meant to encourage anyone to violate the law. I am a strong believer in following the legal obligations imposed on us by our various governments, be they federal, state or local. If I disagree with a certain law, I will work to change it, but I won't violate it.

Of course, if, God forbid, society collapses, and the government and its laws simply come to an end, then all bets are off. In a true SHTF situation, you should protect yourself and your loved ones within the Higher Law, or whatever set of morals you live by. Until then, I encourage you to follow the law, and nothing in this book is meant to be construed otherwise.

There are six traditionally-recognized areas of survival: food, water, shelter, security, first aid, and sanitation. This book will help you achieve the survival goal of having a secure shelter, which will be your survival retreat. Working with your survival retreat will be a long process, and in reality, may never fully come to an end. But your journey will begin when you turn the page and proceed with this book.

Let's get started!

Chapter 1

The Numbers

I know what you're thinking: "You rich preppers, spending so much on your retreat properties ... must be nice." But it's a lot cheaper than you might think. When you have lived your whole life in a city or suburban area, you become accustomed to higher land prices, and higher costs per square foot. But that is not the case for raw land in the country. Far from it.

Below I include my research on ten American cities, in which I compare the average house price inside the city with 20-50 acres of non-commercial raw land, without a house, in areas that are at least 100 miles outside the listed city. My numbers are not exact, and I arbitrarily pick communities that are 100 miles away from the city in question. I did all this research in early 2017. Also, my sources are included, so you can do this research yourself if you wish.

The point here is that it is a lot cheaper than you may think to buy a retreat property of 20 to 50 acres for your survival retreat.

Atlanta: Average house price: $200,000, according to Zillow.com. Lots in Etowah County, Alabama, sell for an average of $165,000 (per landandfarm.com). Reverse sticker-shock: 18% discount.

Chicago: Average house price: $212,000, according to Zillow.com. Lots in Janesville, Wisconsin, sell for an average of $139,000 (per realtor.com). Reverse sticker-shock: 34% discount.

Denver: Average house price: $366,000, according to Zillow.com. Lots in Lake County, Colorado, sell for an average of $79,000 (per landwatch.com). Reverse sticker-shock: 78% discount.

Houston: Average house price: $230,000, according to Houston Chronicle, July 13, 2016. Lots in Houston County, Texas, sell for an average of $133,000 (per landsoftexas.com). Reverse sticker-shock: 42% discount.

Los Angeles: Average house price: $603,000, according to Zillow.com. Lots in the Coachella Valley sell for an average of $80,000 (per landandfarm.com). Reverse sticker-shock: 86% discount.

New York City: Average condominium price: $916,000, according to *New York Times* January 16, 2015. Lots in between Syracuse and Saratoga Springs, New York, sell for an average of $82,000 (per landandfarm.com). Reverse sticker-shock: 91% discount.

Orlando: Average house price: $160,000, according to Zillow.com. Lots in Taylor County, Florida, sell for an average of $114,000 (per landandfarm.com). Reverse sticker-shock: 29% discount.

San Francisco: Average house price: $1.1 million, according to Zillow.com. Lots in Lake County, California, sell for an average of $210,000 (per landsofamerica.com). Reverse sticker-shock: 81% discount.

Seattle: Average house price: $612,000, according to Zillow.com. Lots in Walla Walla County, Washington, sell for an average of $210,000 (per landandfarm.com). Reverse sticker-shock: 67% discount.

Washington, D.C.: Average house price: $530,000, according to Zillow.com. Lots in Berkeley Springs, West Virginia, sell for an average price of $157,000. Reverse sticker-shock: 70% discount.

Granted, some of these areas, like Atlanta, Chicago, and Orlando, did not have a giant difference in the home price in the city versus the price of 20 to 50 acres of uncommercial, raw land that was over 100 miles away. But, by and large, the raw land way outside the city is a lot cheaper than the residents of those cities might think. Of all the cities I picked, the average discount, or "reverse sticker-shock" discount of raw land from the price of a home in the city was a whopping 59%!

And I only checked raw land that was 20 – 50 acres. If you look further into the websites I researched, the price per acre for parcels of land that are 100 acres or more is even cheaper!

Maybe you live in an area where a lot of your neighbors have cabins, lake houses or hunting properties outside of the city, and no one thinks it is that expensive. In that situation, you may be conditioned to think that owning a piece of property 100 miles outside of the city is doable and not expensive. Good for you.

But if you have spent most of your life in a city like San Francisco or New York, or another similarly-expensive city, you might be conditioned into thinking that buying a 20 – 50-acre parcel of raw land outside of your city is just not possible. "It might be conceivable for people in those other, more affordable areas, but not for me," you might say.

Well, guess again! Pick a day off, plant your fanny in your car seat and drive 100 miles or more outside of your city and check out the available parcels of raw land out there. You will be amazed at how affordable it is, even for you!

Location

This one is easy, but make sure to stick to a certain philosophy: not only do you want to pay less for a retreat property, which is made more likely when you look for properties 100 miles or more away from your city, but also make sure that your retreat property is complicated to get to. If society collapses and hordes of hungry people leave the city in search of food, you want to make sure that those people go to other properties, and not yours. For example, the properties that are right next to an Interstate highway will be almost immediately descended upon, and those land-owners will find themselves overrun very quickly. Any thoughts that those landowners had of having a secure property in case of societal collapse will have been way off. The properties that are a few roads away from a major highway will be less likely to be targeted by the unprepared.

Here's another consideration, and this is important: you should also look for a property that has a "precarious stretch of road" in an approach to the property. In case of societal collapse, a precarious stretch of road can be destroyed, so that any hordes of hungry city-dwellers will simply not be able to get to your property.

Here are some other examples of what I mean by a precarious stretch of road: a stretch of road that traverses a steep hillside, a road that goes through a forest, or a small bridge. Taken in order, a road that traverses a hillside can be damaged or blocked to make it impassable, trees can be chopped down to block a road through a forest, and a small bridge can be dismantled so that cars or hikers can no longer go across it. That's what the Ray Milland character did in the movie *Panic In Year Zero*, and the characters played by Ray Milland didn't mess around.

Piles of debris that contain chopped down trees and large branches also make good road blocks, even without a precarious stretch of road. Also, marauders will be less likely to try and go through or push aside a roadblock if there is a dead animal or two somewhere in the pile of brush. The bigger the animal, the more gross the smells will come from its rotting body.

Here is another location issue: nuclear power plants, both commercial and research. If you want to get a survival retreat property in order to have a place to escape to in case of nuclear power plants melting down, obviously you should make sure that your survival retreat property is not immediately downwind from a nuclear power plant. Here are a couple of websites that will give maps of the locations of nuclear power plants in the United States: nei.org and nrc.gov.

Not all nuclear power plants are prone to meltdowns. The "pass-through" plants that divert a nearby river to cool down the reactor core are not dependent on outside power to stay cool. But keep this in mind: if a tsunami could cause a meltdown at a nuclear reactor in Japan, one of the most technologically-advanced countries on Earth, it can happen everywhere. Reportedly, as of the writing of this book, Japan's Fukushima Daiichi nuclear plant is still emitting nuclear fallout downwind.

It also might be a good idea to keep on hand a good supply of potassium iodide pills. I have found a set of 14 pills (admittedly not yet tested) on Amazon for $8.

Proximity to water is also an important location issue. A property that has a stream or river going through it or nearby is much more usable as a survival retreat. Also, it would help to know if the neighbors of any given piece of land have been able to successfully drill water wells. If the property you are considering is in an area where *no one* has been able to get a good water well in, then you would want to look for your property elsewhere.

Due Diligence

When you find a property you are interested in, make sure to get the owner's permission to walk the property, and if there is a realtor involved, ask the realtor for as many details as you can get on the property. You should also view the parcel and topographical maps, which are available from the realtor or at the county land office.

By personally viewing the property, you can be assured that there are no other problems with it, like chemical waste or excessive trash that must be removed at great expense, or slow-draining areas that government officials will someday claim is a "wetland." In one of my searches for raw land, I once came across a parcel that looked as if it were jam-packed with junked cars, literally as far as the eye could see. No doubt I would have been asked to remove all these cars if I had bought that property. I also once saw a parcel of land that seemed to have an average angle of 45 degrees everywhere on the parcel, so that land was not very usable in any practical sense. It would also be a good idea to make sure that the property has at least enough flat areas to accommodate a driveway that could someday lead to a home-building site.

It would also be a good idea to look into (or ask a realtor) whether the property has any animals on the property that would stop you from building or developing the property. The federal government has many animals listed as either "threatened" or "endangered" that would slow down or stop any development on the property. You can check the federal database at this website: https://www.fws.gov/endangered/ . Many states have similar laws, and the lists of animals that are considered threatened or endangered by the states are not always the same as those by the federal government. A good place to start checking your state's list of protected animals would be to Google "fish and wildlife office" (or similar name) in your state.

Financing

Another pleasant surprise you might experience in shopping for property in the country is that a lot of properties for sale will be offered with owner financing. The seller-financer will want to cover themselves, so don't be surprised if they ask for 10% down, an interest rate higher than the going market rate, and a payment plan of only ten years.

You will also need to clear up any IRS tax liens and any hiccups that are on your credit record. For help clearing up problems on my credit record, I was happy that I hired the online law firm, Lexington Law (lexingtonlaw.com). And while they are not law firms, I have heard good things about the credit repair services thecreditpeople.net and skybluecredit.com. All of these credit repair services challenge negative notifications on your credit record, and if the credit reporter involved does not answer correctly, or on time, the ding on your credit record gets removed. After a credit repair service works on your credit for few months, it is possible to have a mediocre credit report cleaned up so that the rating will be above 700, the approximate number that convinces lenders and property owners that you are a good risk for a mortgage.

Have A Plan B

In all of life's endeavors, it is good to have a "Plan B," so that if you are unsuccessful at what you try to do, there will be a back-up plan to still make your actions worthwhile. You know, some way of breaking even or even getting ahead a different way if you are not successful your first approach.

When it comes to buying a survival retreat, keep in mind that if this property is never needed for its intended purpose – if you never need to escape a societal collapse – the property may still be valuable someday as an investment property. In fact, it could be that someday, the property you had intended to be a retreat property becomes a large part of your net worth in a society that has *not* collapsed.

I would encourage you to keep this in mind: there is no way of predicting the future, and the relative stability that our country has known for many years may very well continue. Who knows? Society might not collapse as planned. Keep this in mind when you shop for your retreat property.

Think about buying a property in a location where it might someday appreciate in value, so you can sell it if you don't have to survive on it.

Where to buy such a property? Many books, seminars, and college courses, each with a cost of their own, have sought to answer this question. And of course, such an in-depth treatment would be outside the scope of a book on survival retreats.

But here is a success story, from a person everyone knows: Bob Hope. Throughout his entertainment career, Bob Hope invested his acting income in real estate on the outskirts of communities that were growing. At one point, Hope owned thousands of acres in Malibu, Beverly Hills, and Palm Springs, California, and also in Phoenix, Arizona. All of these properties were bought at a time when these communities were not widely-known or even inhabited. In 1939, Hope bought a house on five acres in Toluca Lake, California, at a time when Toluca Lake was just a dusty, remote location, about twenty miles north of Hollywood. Nowadays, Toluca Lake is surrounded by the suburbia of the San Fernando Valley area of Los Angeles, and Bob Hope's house was recently listed for sale there for $12 million.

If Bob Hope were alive today, a prepper of modest means (like you and I), and looking for a retreat property, he would probably look for some property that had all the qualities necessary to sustain him and his family in case of a societal collapse. But he would also make sure that his property would be in an area of the country with good growth potential. That way, if society stayed intact, he would have a back-up plan to sell the property for a nice profit. And, as he signed the closing paperwork that formalized his nice profit in selling the property, he would probably be singing "Thanks For The Memory" to himself!

I call this "Plan B, for Bob Hope." Buy a good survival retreat that has all the qualities described in this book, outside of a growing metropolitan area. If the property is never needed as a retreat location, someday you could sell it for a big profit.

Chapter 2
Land-Locked Property

As you search for parcels of raw land in the area that interests you, you may come across a seemingly-too-good bargain: an asking price for a piece of land that makes you scratch your head and think, "This can't be."

And, of course, as you look further into the property and its details, you find that it is indeed too good a deal to be true. See, sometimes properties out on the country are put on the market, and they are -- get this – inaccessible from the public road. That's right! Someone will list a property for sale that cannot be gotten to unless you first drive or hike through a neighbor's property. Or you can hitch a ride on a helicopter, or maybe take up pole-vaulting.

In such a situation, once you find out that this is the case with a piece of property, you will feel disappointed, because you spent time getting excited about the property, then found out about its fatal flaw.

But think again. This might be a great buying opportunity, in disguise.

Any inaccessible property is actually an accessible property once it has an easement road gotten from a neighbor. And easement roads are always possible.

First, let me present a couple of legal issues, and these are only meant to whet your appetite. If you find yourself tempted to buy a piece of property where this is an issue, you should first consult a real estate attorney licensed in the state of the property in question (*see* Additional Resources for self-help law books that might help, or Appendix II on how to deal with attorneys). Such a local real estate attorney will be able to explain all this stuff to you, and will probably be able to help you.

And don't be intimidated by consulting or hiring an attorney. In fact, don't be intimidated by anything. A lot of goals in life are do-able if only you can remind yourself that the goal can be done.

Now, on to the legal issues: an "easement" is a legal right to use or travel through part of someone else's property. An easement can be prescriptive, meaning it was taken away involuntarily from the landowner or granted, meaning that the landowner gave or sold the easement. For example, power companies often purchase easements from landowners so that the power company can construct and maintain power poles that go through a property, bringing electricity to other properties far away.

Properties that are nearby a beach can often be the scene of prescriptive easements. When members of a community regularly walk through a beach-front property for some years to get to the beach, without permission, the community as a whole may get a prescriptive easement declared by a court. I think something like this happened to a beach house that John Candy's character rented in the movie *Summer Rental*. After moving his family into a beautiful, secluded beach house one afternoon, the next morning John Candy's family was annoyed to see hundreds of people walk through the property, right next to their dining room, on their way to the beach. It was a pretty funny scene.

So, here's the thing: if, during your search for raw land, you find a very inexpensive property that is for sale, but is not accessible to a public road unless you walk or drive through someone else's property, you should look into the possibility of buying an easement road from the owner of the property between your possible property and the nearby public road. An easement road would allow you to drive from the public road, through the neighboring property, to the property that you want to buy.

Here is how it could happen:

Step one: you see an excellent property that is unusually cheap for what you think you get. Sometimes an advertisement of the available property mentions this pesky issue, but I have seen flyers and ads of properties where this minor detail is not mentioned at all.

Step two: after checking, you find that this property cannot be gotten to from the public road unless you first hike or drive through a neighboring property. Add to it this sometimes-tantalizing legal red-herring: the neighboring property owner tells you, "No problem. You can hike or drive through my property anytime you want to. I've been good friends with this property owner for ages." Don't be tempted! This oral promise is not as good as the paper it isn't written on!

Step three: contact the owner of the property between the property you are interested in and the public road. Tell the property owner that you would like to check out the land-locked property that is for sale, but that you would like the outside property owner's permission before hiking to the land-locked property, just to "keep it legal." After a conversation or two, the subject might mosey on over (that's country-speak for "progress to…") what a buyer of the land-locked property could do to make permanent access legal, and how much an easement road would cost.

Step four: contact a local real estate attorney (often through the local county bar association's lawyer referral service), and ask the attorney, "What steps should I take to get a legal and permanent easement road, for all my anticipated uses, through the neighboring property?" The attorney might suggest that you approach the neighboring property and offer to buy an "option" for an easement road before you try to buy the inaccessible property. Such an option may specify an approximate route, using longitude and latitude readings from a handheld GPS unit, specify a width of at least 40 feet, include the fact that the easement would be permanent, any limits of use of the easement road (ideally, none), and the easement price that will be paid once you buy the target property.

Step five: if you can get an easement option agreed upon and paid to the neighboring property owner, you then must make an offer to the owner of the heretofore-landlocked property. Whether to admit to this landowner that the accessibility issue is resolved or not is something you should discuss with your attorney. Don't be surprised if the asking price of the target property goes up once the landowner finds out that the property is not as inaccessible as he or she thought. Land-locked property is usually offered at a discount for a reason.

Step six: in all goes according to plan, you have paid for an option for a permanent easement road, and you have bought or entered into a contract to buy the inside parcel of land. You will probably find that the price for *both* the easement road *and* the property is much less than what you would have paid for with a similar property in that area without any accessibility issues. Also, both documents, the easement deed document (after you follow through on the option and buy the easement) and the deed of sale of the property, must be signed in front of a notary and filed with the county where the land is located. The only catch was that you had to go through the hassle of contacting an attorney and working all this out.

Also, keep in mind that many times an attorney will offer up to thirty minutes of free initial consultation at the beginning, so you can see if you are on the right track. Real estate attorneys have an incentive to charge reasonable fees because a new property owner might be a client in any future real estate legal issues.

Here's another detail to be aware of: if you can buy an easement road from the owner of the property between your property and the nearest public road, make sure that the easement-seller actually owns his or her property outright. If there is a mortgage on that property, you will need to get the formal approval of the mortgage owner as well as the person who says he is the owner of that property.

Oh, and one other thing: some jurisdictions have rules governing the point at which the easement road intersects with the public road. Sometimes an easement road must intersect at a roughly ninety-degree angle, and often the road must be a certain number of feet away from any other intersection or turn in the public road.

But be careful with inaccessible property. If you are interested in a beautiful, inexpensive survival retreat property that is inaccessible, and you cannot get an easement road or buy the property between this property and the nearest road, my advice would be for you to just walk away from it. Don't buy it! That friendly neighbor who informally allows you to drive or hike across his property to get to your property might change his mind, or die, and his family will revoke the access. Then, the property will be effectively worthless, and all the money you spent on it will have been a waste. I have seen it happen.

On the other hand, if you can link an inaccessible property with a public road by getting an easement road from the neighbor, you will have gotten a nice survival retreat at a huge discount from the nearby properties. No doubt there was some hassle, and you may have had to work with an attorney, but it was well worth it. If there were no hassle involved, everyone would do this, and there would be no discount.

Chapter 3
Foreclosure Auctions

Buying property at a foreclosure auction is one method of buying a survival retreat as cheaply as possible, which is the focus of this book. And although I cannot say that I have ever pulled the trigger on buying a house or a piece of property at a foreclosure auction, I have been to a ton of them.

If, during your search for a survival retreat, you find a particular county that you would like to buy land in, and you are interested in property auctions there, go by the office or check out the website of that county's sheriff. If the county is lightly-populated, there won't be much on their website, and there will be a paper list of foreclosed properties and the intended auction dates for those properties on the wall near the front door of the sheriff's office. If the county is more populated, there might be a whole office within the sheriff that is devoted to auctioning off foreclosed properties, and the sheriff's website would be more helpful.

When the date and time comes to auction the list of properties (and other things, like cars or trucks that have been announced for auction), a sheriff employee will just stand in front of the sheriff's office, or wherever the auction is announced, and the auction will occur among a handful of people who are standing nearby. You may be surprised at how informal it all is.

Sometimes a bank will have a huge lien on the property up for auction, and a representative from the bank will bid the amount of the lien to buy the property. Believe it or not, banks are not too smart in handling properties that they own, so if you later check with that same bank, you might be able to offer to buy the property for less than the lien amount. Your offer might just be accepted!

Some county sheriffs outsource their property auctions to auction companies. A Google check would reveal if this is what happens with the county you like. The auction company will also get a cut of the money raised at the auction, so it will typically promote the auction to bring in more bidders.

I admit it, I am not too keen on property auctions, for several reasons. Here is my top reason: rarely is it possible to do a thorough due-diligence search of a property up for auction. Mostly it is because the "contact" person listed is not helpful or even available. Sometimes a realtor is listed as a contact for the property, and the realtor doesn't know much about it. The estate of a deceased person far away could list as a contact for the property, and you will not be able to find out anything. Sometimes the previous owner of the property is listed, and he or she is too grumpy to get on the phone and give out any information about the property.

So how do you check out the property? How would you know, for example, if some horrible chemical has been dumped on this property, requiring costly removal?

What do you do if you cannot find anyone around who could grant you access to the property? Going onto the property without the permission of someone in charge of it could be dangerous and illegal, so I would definitely not recommend it. What if the former property owner still claims the property, and has a few pit bulls there, ready to devour any trespassers?

You could call a local realtor and ask if they would be willing to fax or e-mail you "comparables" of nearby properties. This would give you an idea of what nearby properties have sold for, and how long ago. Also, getting a parcel map from a realtor or the county land office may reveal if the property is not accessible to a local road (and if that is the case, re-read the chapter in this book on land-locked properties).

Other things to look for may include a possible squatter, who doesn't care who thinks they own the land up for auction. There could also be a hiking trail that goes right through the middle of this property, and the trail could later be claimed in court as a permanent prescriptive easement. What if there is a group of people illegally camping on the property, growing marijuana? Believe it or not, I have seen each of these very circumstances on properties that were up for auction.

Here's another thing: if the former property owner comes up with the money owed on this property, the auction for that property would be canceled. You would then have wasted a lot of time checking out that property.

Before you even go to an auction, you will need to find out how much money, and in what form, will be required to pay if you win the auction for that property. Will you have to pay 100% of the bid price right after the auction, or 10% then and the remainder within three days? And will you need a bank cashier's check, or is a personal check possible? If you have to get a cashier's check for the auction and you *don't* win the auction on that property, then you will be returning to your bank to get a refund on your cashier's check and pay the bank's fees. Hassling with cashier's checks and getting refunds on them after not winning an auction is another complaint I have had about land auctions.

Of course, carrying a cashier's check is better than walking around with lots of cash. I once went to a property auction that was held inside a courthouse, so all the bidders had to first go through a metal detector. There were several people I noticed who walked in with briefcases, and because of how they handled their briefcases I was convinced that there was a lot of cash inside. Call me paranoid, but I would never advise walking around town with more than a few thousand dollars cash like I think those people did.

But if you do find yourself in a crowd of people, bidding for properties at an auction, I have noticed a correlation as far as low relative winning bids versus time of the auction. In my opinion, there are parts of the auction where the best deals are to be had.

Sure, this is a loose correlation and does not happen at every auction. But this is what I have noticed: the first 10% of the auction gets the highest relative bids. People are excited to be there, and they are eager to bid and win. The beginning of an auction is also the time of the auction when everyone there has the most money.

After this initial bidding frenzy, the bids relative to the value of the properties auctioned trend downward until about the final 10% of the auction. At that time, the bidders realize that the auction is about to end, so they refocus their bidding to buy something so that they won't have wasted their time going to the auction. The prices go back up at the end of the auction.

In my opinion, after having sat through many property auctions, I believe that the best deals are when the auction is about 50% to 75% over. At that point, the excitement has died down, maybe some boredom has set in, the early parts of the auction have depleted the money of other bidders there, and the bidders have not yet realized that the auction is almost over.

What this means is that if you find some properties that you would be willing to bid on, you will probably find that the best auction prices happen when the auction is half- to three-quarters over. And, as I wrote, this is what I have noticed most of the time.

It would be a good idea to attend several property auctions before you attend one in which you will seriously bid on a piece of property. You may find that property auctions call for too much money, and the unknowns of what you are bidding on are too much.

Chapter 4
Google Earth

If this book had any background music while you read it, the music would suddenly turn somber and foreboding as you read this chapter. For better or worse, Google has changed a lot about life as we know it in the United States, and Google Earth, and its more navigationally-relevant Google Maps, have for the most part ended privacy here.

One of the things I always valued about my property in the country was the sense of privacy I felt when I was there. Not that I wanted to walk around in the nude or anything, but I really cherished the feeling of being way out in the country, not being noticed by *anyone*. All by myself. Then one day my wife showed me the image that Google Earth showed of our property. It was quite a shock!

In my estimate, Google Earth shows the details of our property from an altitude of about 200 feet up. And Google seems to update its image every year or two. One day, a couple of years back, we had on our property a certain white truck, parked at a specific location. We also had one of our friends visiting, and he brought with him his little white dog. Both the truck and the little dog appear on the latest Google Earth image of our property. The rest of our property, with our tools and various pieces of equipment, were clearly seen on Google Earth.

This has many implications. It used to be that government officials had to try and trespass on a piece of property to see what was going on there. Now they just log onto Google Earth and input the parcel number. They can even see the previous images posted by Google Earth from last year, two years ago, or however long they want to go back into the history of your property. If they want to, the government officials can see if you are building anything or clearing any land, or doing anything else that would require some kind of permit, or raising the assessed value of your property.

I also think it is just a matter of time before thieves start to use Google Earth. They can look at your property and first, determine whether there is a permanent house there, and then see what is on your land that can be stolen. Farm machinery, ATV's, tools, hoses, generators, even patio furniture can be seen from Google Earth and inform enterprising thieves.

What about the unprepared, who look for places to take over if SHTF? What is to stop them from utilizing Google Earth to make a list of local places to be taken over in case of a societal collapse? Nothing.

I place this precautionary chapter here so that you can plan accordingly. For one, anything valuable, like an ATV, should be hidden from view. Tools and generators should be locked to, or inside of, something that cannot be stolen. Google Earth cannot see through trees, so any trees that are dying or just "in the way" of a project should be left in place until the last possible moment.

It is also a good idea to start making sure that whatever is left on your property is camouflage in color, either naturally or painted that way. Rust-Oleum sells some great camouflage green or tan spray paint that is very useful. The last time I saw some at the local Walmart, it went for $4 a can.

For the extra paranoid landowner, camouflage ghillie netting, available online, matched as best as possible to the geography of your land, can be used to cover up larger items. Ghillie netting will conceal items from Google Earth, but can also hide shadows on the sides of items that have any amount of height to them.

As of the printing of this book, Google Earth is a free computer program that anyone can download to their computer or smart phone. If you download the program and play around on it a while, you will see that there are many details on your property that are simply not private anymore.

I have read many articles written on "hiding" a piece of property from Google Earth, but I remain very skeptical. Offthegridnews.com and survivalistboards.com have wrestled with the issue, but so far as I can tell, only the federal government can get any property really hidden from Google Earth.

Even though your property can be seen on Google Earth, if it were possible to hide anything on your property from Google Earth, it certainly is within your rights to do so. Unless you consent or somehow sign away your rights, you still have a Fourth Amendment constitutional right against a warrantless, unreasonable search and seizure. And the government does not have a permanent warrant to snoop on your property.

The government is able to look at your property on Google Earth without a warrant because it falls under the "plain view" exception to the Fourth Amendment, just like a police officer standing nearby your car can look onto what is on the front seat inside your car. But there is no legal impediment to hiding your stuff on your own property, just like you are not required to put everything inside your car onto the front seat so that the police officer can see it. You are well within your rights to keep your stuff private, and you should.

Chapter 5
Taxes And Insurance

Once you have bought your retreat property, local property taxes will be based upon the assessed value of your land, and must always be paid. Taxes on raw land will be low because the value of the land is usually assessed low. If you build anything new on your property, like a barn or house, the local government will probably require a permit and "re-assess" the value of your land higher, making your property taxes increase.

The local county property office will be able to tell you the largest shed that you can build without getting a permit or re-assessing the value of the land. Sometimes, the county will allow a shed of a certain size to be built without a permit, but if the shed has any electricity or plumbing in it, the shed will need a permit and trigger a re-assessment of the value of the property.

When you go to the county land-use office (different counties have different names for this office), you can ask about what permits are required for building what projects you have in mind, but you need not go into too much detail with these government employees. It is best to keep it all hypothetical. If they resent the lack of details about your plans or which property is yours, you can remind them, "I just want to find out what the rules are so that I can follow them. That's why I'm here."

You may also find that the county is always looking for excuses to reassess the value of your property higher so that your property tax bill will go up. On the other hand, it is possible to get the value of your property assessed *lower*, which would make your property taxes decrease.

This happened to me: I had a neighbor whose property got foreclosed on and the property next to mine was sold at an auction. I knew the sale price and contacted my county to get my property value assessed lower, to be in line with the "comparables" in my area. And it was true, that I bought my property based upon an approximate dollar-per-acre number in the area, which was now a lot lower. It worked! A couple months later I got a letter from the county, informing me of the lower assessed value of my property, and my lower property tax bill. Cha-ching!

Insurance is another bill that should be paid. If your property is close to houses or any development, you should get liability insurance on the property. This is annoying but true: if anyone trespasses on your property and gets injured, they will sue you. An insurance policy will protect you from that.

And, sure, if you have anything of value on your property, like a barn or a house, they should also be insured against loss.

If you use your raw land for any of the money-making ideas listed in chapter 26, you will need insurance. A lot of those ideas will require someone else to be on your property, without your supervision. In one of those ideas, harvesting timber, people will be operating dangerous equipment, like a chainsaw, not to mention having a tree fall on them, so the potential for injuries and law suits is pretty high. Better be insured.

All this can be a hassle and cost some money, but it may also be a great excuse to keep people off your property, even those who are not immediately suspect. Once, at my property, a neighbor's kid told me that he and a school friend of his were collecting tree branches for a school project, and they requested to go onto my property to collect tree branches there. I wanted to keep relations good with my neighbor, but I did not want the kid on my property checking out what might be there that could be stolen. Or who knows? The kid could have talked to his classmates, who might be tempted to trespass on my property and steal my stuff.

Admittedly, I wasn't too concerned that this kid or his friend would get injured, but I told the kid that my insurance does not cover what he and his friend were doing, and I did not want him to possibly get injured and have a huge hospital bill. Sure, this was all true, but yeah, it was passive.

But hey, it worked. The neighbor immediately understood, and it saved me from having to say, "Get lost, kid!"

Chapter 6
Water, Your New Obsession

In the 1964 movie *Dr. Strangelove*, the character General Jack D. Ripper unilaterally attacked the Soviet Union with over 1,300 megatons of nuclear weapons, and then made some good points about the importance of clean water. "Water is the source of all life," he began. "Seven-tenths of this earth's surface is water. Why, do you realize that 70% of *you* is water? And as human beings, you and I need fresh, pure water to replenish our precious bodily fluids. Are you beginning to understand?"

Who says a mass-murdering psychopath can't occasionally make sense? Ripper offered some good advice here. Water is extremely important to all life. As part of the "Rules of Three," preppers know that the human body dies after three days without water.

I believe that stored water and the ability to get more water and filter it are every prepper's weakest links. If you don't have this issue nailed down for your survival retreat in an SHTF situation, nothing else matters. Whatever else your survival retreat has going for it, if you are without water, everything else you have done for your survival retreat will have been done in vain.

Below I will give some brief advice on water acquisition, storage, and purification. But please do not rely solely on this chapter for these important topics. Adequately covering all the different subjects of water would require a separate book.

First, on the subject of acquiring water, keep a look out for a creek, river or lake that is on or runs through the property when you consider which properties to buy. Property that has a ready water source is much more valuable to you.

You may want to drill a water well on your property, and before you do so, ask neighbors if the water table is within reach. Some states offer a free geological survey of your land, suggesting the best locations on a parcel to drill for water.

The installation of a water well can be expensive, sometimes costing $10,000 or more. In many areas, a permit is required to drill a water well, but the well driller can get the permit for you and include it in the cost of your well. If you are able to, it would be best to drill a well at a higher elevation, so that you can easily direct the water into water tanks downhill that will be used by your house or for irrigation.

Also, make sure that the hole of the completed well has enough of a diameter to accommodate not only the pipe for a manual water pump (those cost around $1,500) but also the pipe for a motorized pump (solar-powered pumps often go for $2,000 on up), and maybe even the pipe of a windmill (which costs at least $1,500). This is like a milkshake with two or more straws in it.

The area where the well comes out of the ground needs to be protected from surface water collecting and seeping back down the water well hole. This is called runoff contamination. You might notice many water wells have a small concrete slab put there to protect the well from runoff.

A nearby latrine, septic system, or livestock pen would also contaminate your well, so you should drill your well at least 75-100 feet away from them.

If the local government allows you to drill your water well, you should educate yourself on how to do it, and what equipment is for sale out there. YouTube is the best place to find such equipment for sale because you can see how the equipment works.

Once you have a completed water well, you can have water samples tested to see if there are too many minerals in the water, and what can be done to rectify the issue. A water softening system might be needed to make the water drinkable, and non-corrosive for the water pipes.

Secondly, the storing of water is also important. There are several options available, but the cheapest and most available are the green or black polyethylene tanks sold by farm equipment stores (a 3,000-gallon tank usually sells for around $1,100). These tanks keep out the sun so that algae does not grow in the water. It is also a good idea to install a water filter between the tank of your dwelling and to protect the spigot from the tank and bury the water pipes deep enough so that a frost will not destroy them.

Ideally, you will have a water tank installed uphill from your dwelling so that the water will flow into your house. An elevation of 100 feet higher than your house will yield 43 pounds-per-square-inch water pressure, which is an acceptable pressure for most houses. If you have level land or for whatever reason cannot get a 100-foot elevation for your stored water, you will need to get a water pump.

And finally, I also wanted to include some thoughts on personal water storage and purification. With nothing more than a manual water pump on a well, or collecting water from a stream, river, or lake, you may need to just keep your water in a smaller container, like a 5-gallon bucket. The most reliable way of purifying water is to boil it for one minute.

You may also choose to filter the water, and for this, I would recommend the Berkey line of water filter products. Berkey sells a "Big Berkey," which is a counter-top tank and filter that holds as much as three gallons of water and filters out contaminants and fluoride so that the water tastes great. For Berkey products, I have found that Directiv21.com has the best prices, but Amazon is close behind.

I also like the "Sports Berkey" 22-ounce water filter bottle, which allows you to collect water outdoors and filter it when you drink it. Amazon sells these for $29 apiece. Other companies that sell impressive personal water filters include Sawyer, Katadyn, and Water Straw. All of these products have filters that must the replaced from time to time.

Whether in a huge water tank or in a smaller container, it is also accepted to purify water by adding into the water drops of bleach. Here is a good rule of thumb on how to remember the amount of bleach to add to water to purify it: water weighs eight pounds per gallon. Well, purifying water with bleach takes eight drops of bleach per gallon of water. Isn't that easy?

The main problem with bleach is that when you buy it in the store, it is already in the process of degrading, and will lose all of its potency in a matter of months. Pool shock can be stored and turned into bleach. But be careful, pool shock can be dangerous. I spent a lot of time on converting pool shock to bleach in my last prepping book, *Dirt Cheap Valuable Prepping*.

Chapter 7

Restroom Issues

Let's face it: many outdoor-types can go to the restroom *anywhere*. But not everyone operates that way. Some people need a lot of something known as "privacy," when going to the restroom.

If you hope to get someone to your survival retreat who values their privacy, then you will need some kind of enclosed restroom, ready to be used at a moment's notice. You have several options.

For most survivalists or off-grid people, that means getting a composting toilet. The principle of a composting toilet is simple: it is a toilet on top of an electrical composter. The sewage goes to a composter that heats and churns the sewage until it becomes ash.

The first time I saw a composting toilet, I thought it was a throne. And sure enough, many of them do look like thrones. Others look like normal toilets, and a separate composter is in the floor below the toilet.

Here are the main brands and starting prices of some composting toilets:

Sun-Mar (at sun-mar.com from $1700)
Envirolet (at envirolet.com from $2100)
Biolet (at biolet.com starting at $1250)
Nature's Head (on Amazon.com or natureshead.net from $960)

With all composting toilets, a vent from the toilet to the roof, as straight as possible, is critical. Otherwise, you should use a lot of sawdust or cat litter in the composter to keep the smell in check.

For composting toilets and the parts they need, you should check bensdiscountsupply.com, thenaturalhome.com, and lehmans.com.

I admit to having some skepticism about composting toilets. Most of them smell bad. We once had a composting toilet, and we managed. I have seen others that smell like sewage, or if they don't, their sewage smell is covered up by an overpowering ammonia smell put there to cover up the sewage smell. Also, some parts of the country don't even allow composting toilets.

For a restroom on your property, you could also build an outhouse or latrine. This is basically a small shed with a toilet seat above a hole in the floor so that your waste goes into a hole dug in the ground below. Assuming latrines are legal where your property is, you should check the soil around the latrine before you build it. You want soil that will absorb liquids, which is called "percolating." If you build a latrine above soil that is mostly clay, the sewage will not go anywhere and will just sit there, attracting flies and just being totally gross. Another thing I would advise about latrines is that you periodically pour Rid-X down the hole. Rid-X, available at Walmart for $14, is a powder of bacteria and enzymes that break down sewage. You could also drop into the hole some RV holding tank deodorizers. Believe it or not, I have seen some relatively odor-free latrines.

Or you could buy a porta-potty. They start at about $530 on EBay nowadays, and the brand I saw was Polyjohn (porta-potties always seem to have these humorous names!).

Or you could do what I did a few years ago: I made a porta-potty on wheels. I called around and bought a porta-potty (they weren't available on EBay back then). The porta-potty salesman told me that he was used to contractors buying them. It cost me about $1000, but I got the additional urinal and foot-pump hand-washing sink inside.

Porta-potties have a tub beneath the toilet that collects the sewage, and the porta-potty owner typically pays a sewage pumping service to come by once a month to suck out the sewage.

In my case, I drilled a drain hole in the bottom of the porta-potty sewage tank; then I attached the porta-potty onto a very small utility trailer. Then, I set up a sewage hose hook-up on the side, like what you might have with an RV, connected to the hole in the bottom of the sewage tank. When the sewage tank fills up, I drain it into a portable sewage tank on wheels that I bought on EBay for $30. Then I transport and dump the sewage into a latrine, RV sewage dump at an RV park, or just into the sewer cleanout at my house.

I also keep on hand some RV holding tank deodorizers that I bought at Walmart for $10 for a package of 10. These are meant for RV black water holding tanks, but they also work for my porta-potty.

I also welded a foldable steel, RV trailer step on the back. After its completion, I was so proud of this thing that I towed it around town, at a slow speed, with my window down. That way, if anyone wanted to ask me about it, I could easily pull over and explain all the details of this magnificent invention.

The trucks of a lot of farm workers tow around their porta-potty too, but they are filled with sewage, and they have to be sucked out every once in a while. I can drain mine without having to drive it anywhere.

I experienced a setback when I inquired at the office of motor vehicles what I needed to do to license this system, which was really a trailer. The woman there told me that they don't register these trailers. I asked about possibly getting a citation for towing an unlicensed trailer and was told that most of the time these trailers are towed such short distances, the police don't care.

Also, you cannot drive porta-potties around very fast, as the walls are made of pretty thin plastic, and the wind can make them bend.

If I ever do this again, I might make these changes: buy a porta-potty on EBay but just ditch the toilet and sewage tank, and replace it all with a small composting toilet (with a vent up through the roof). A solar panel on the roof could power the composter.

Another option is to buy a bigger trailer (which would need a trailer's license plate) and attach to it a handicap-sized porta-potty. Those things are huge! I could use the toilet and tank that came with it. But with the extra space inside, I would set up a shower of some sort. A tank of water could be collected, and a solar panel on the roof could power an RV water heater and an RV shower. Instead of the shower water draining into the sewage tank, a separate "gray water" drain could just go out onto the ground or into a separate drainage tank.

The main benefit to any of these porta-potties on wheels is that you can hook it up and tow it to whatever property you need it at. If you sell your survival retreat, you can hook up your porta-potty and move it to your next property. And so on.

Of course, the portability of such a system is a disadvantage, because thieves may also choose to hook up your porta-potty and drive off with it. However, the chances of your porta-potty being stolen are relatively low: I have *never* seen a porta-potty for sale at a pawn shop or swap meet.

But who are we kidding? Thieves will steal anything. Best to hook up a bicycle U-shaped lock around one of the wheels of this trailer.

One last issue I would like to discuss concerning toilets and "the restroom issue" at your survival retreat: toilet paper. If you store some toilet paper in an emergency bag or in your car, make sure to gently separate and discard the inner cardboard cylinder, so that you can squeeze the toilet paper roll into a quart-size freezer baggie. That way, you can keep several rolls in a small space.

You can also store a lot of toilet paper at your survival retreat, but rats could get into the toilet paper and have a grand time. That happened to me once, and I never knew there were that many rats in the whole county, much less my property!

So, if you store a lot of toilet paper, make sure it is very secure from animals.

Here is another idea: the travel bidet. Anyone who has been to Europe has probably stayed at a hotel room that has a bidet next to the toilet. Essentially, a bidet is meant to spray water to your underside, instead of toilet paper. It does a better job than toilet paper of cleaning up down there, but you have to sit in place a little longer so that the water dries up. Just bring a book or magazine with you and the time will fly right by,

Another thing: while toilet paper is finite, meaning that you may run out of it someday, a travel bidet can be used forever, or until it breaks. I have several of these on my property. They can be found at Walmart.com or Amazon for $14.

Chapter 8
Roads

I thought I would spend some time on how to put together a road or driveway on your survival retreat property.

Once you have a point at which you want a driveway to connect with the public road (sometimes this might require a driveway permit), and an area further into your property where you will build a dwelling or have a main assembly area, you will have a road that will connect the two. (See also Chapter 9, regarding the importance of a front gate.)

If your property is flat, no problem. Connect the front gate to your main assembly area, dodging whatever trees or other obstructions are in between, and start working on a road.

If your property is hilly, whether it is by using a topographical map or just by looking around your property while hiking, your road needs to be slightly uphill along the side of the hill, and it also needs to have switchbacks that are not too steep. (In my advice here, I assume your property goes *up* from the front gate. If your property goes down, reverse my advice as appropriate.) In topographical map terms, any switchback needs to be at an area on the map where the topographical lines are relatively far apart. At that area, you can turn the road back with an easy slope, then keep going slightly uphill until there is a need for another switchback further up. You don't want a switchback on your driveway that is very steep because it is difficult for big trucks, like water well-drilling trucks, or any vehicle that is towing a trailer.

With my property, my wife and I first got some pruning shears and yellow plastic trail tape from Home Depot, and we created a hiking trail through the forest, beginning at our front gate. We did our best to keep the trail level to slightly uphill, without any switchbacks that were too steep. Eventually, the trail made it to a large flat area. As time went on, we cleared more brush on either side of the hiking trail, so that it was wide enough to drive a car on it and not have the sides of the car scratched by the branches of nearby trees. Then, we hired a local bull-dozer guy, who made the road pretty smooth, and he even pushed further back the trees on either side of the trail. In some jurisdictions, clearing a hiking trail like this may require a permit. Also, check ahead to Chapter 17 and consider whether you might prefer instead to buy and have delivered your own heavy equipment, like a backhoe, so that you can do all this work yourself. You never know if the bull-dozer operator you hire might have a big mouth, and tell others that you have a vacant piece of land that has a lot of stuff on it that can be stolen.

Now that you have a road that has had the trees and bushes cleared away from it, and it is cleared in such a way that most cars can easily drive on it, it is time to start bringing in gravel and dig drainage ditches. When the rains come, gravel will keep your road from becoming a giant slipping slide, and the ditches will channel the rain so that it doesn't wash away part of your driveway, or create areas on your road where your car could get stuck.

Most areas in the country have gravel pits or businesses that will deliver a dump truck-full of gravel. Most of the time they will only deliver to your front gate, which is a pain if you don't have your own backhoe. Don't be surprised if a truckload of gravel costs $200 or more. For the first few loads of gravel that you spread on your road, the larger and cheaper rocks are fine. When the gravel on your road begins to pack itself in, you should order the smaller rocks for the final applications of gravel.

However you get the gravel onto your road, here is the general philosophy with gravel: with each successive rain that comes along, the gravel on your road will be pushed further and further down into the ground, requiring you to apply yet more layers of gravel onto the same road. At some point, your gravel will hit something below the road (bedrock or whatever) that will stop the gravel from sinking any further. Keep applying more gravel on this road so that the gravel will sink no further, no matter how much rain the road gets or how much it is driven At that point, you apply the final layer of gravel, and the road is packed firm with gravel that will stay in place. This gravel road is now so packed with gravel that an expensive asphalt road will barely be an improvement!

And here is the ideal cross-section that you want with a gravel road: the middle of the road needs to be the highest, gently sloping downward to the outer-most part of the road, so that the rain will not collect in the road and instead flow into the ditches on both sides.

And speaking of ditches, they need to be dug six inches to a foot lower than the outer-most part of the road. In time, dirt or rocks may begin to fill the ditches, so make sure you use a shovel and keep them empty.

Culverts should be used at switchbacks or wherever the possibility exists for a large pool of water to collect on the side of the road. A culvert is a large black plastic or galvanized steel tube, bought from a nearby farm or ranch-supply store, that is placed in a hole dug across the road, to get the water from the ditch on the uphill side of your road to the dirt on the downhill side. After placing the culvert in the hole, the dirt from the road is put back on top of the culvert so that it can be driven over again. I prefer black plastic culverts of at least one foot in diameter because the smaller-diameter culverts I have used have gotten filled up with rocks and dirt, making them useless.

One last thing about roads: if you have a creek on your property, it may become necessary to build a bridge so that your road can extend further into the property beyond the creek. Some jurisdictions are pretty touchy about this, so ask around how it is legally done in your area. If it is possible to place a culvert down, so that the creek goes through the culvert and your road goes over it, try and get a culvert that has a much higher-diameter than needed. That way, if there is a huge rainstorm, you won't have to worry about your bridge being washed away by the creek.

The most expensive bridge option is also the most legal because it does not touch the creek bed: a flat railway car. There are businesses that operate in hilly areas of the country, where you can hire someone to first, pour concrete foundations on both sides of a creek, then lower and bolt into place an old, flat railway car. Those brides are pretty cool, but the last time I got an estimate for one of them on my property it was over $15,000.

Chapter 9
Front Gate

Once you have a driveway in place so that you can drive into and out of your property, keep this thought in mind: government officials and thieves (am I redundant here?) will also appreciate its convenience. The driveway will be a big help to them, and it will enable them to also get onto your property.

It may be difficult to believe this, but government officials will sometimes see an open driveway and just drive in, looking for new structures on the property so that the property value can be assessed higher, or projects that should have had a permit, or whatever. If they are caught, they might say that they wanted to contact you for some reason, and they could not get hold of you at your phone number of record. If a thief is caught driving onto your property, they will act as if they just innocently took a wrong turn. Both groups assume that if they are caught trespassing on your property, nothing will happen to them. And you know what? Usually, they're right.

(If you are especially ballsy, when you encounter a trespasser on your property, consider pulling out your cell phone and photograph them and their car's license plate, and try to get their name and date of birth. Then you can report them to the local sheriff and ask that they be prosecuted for criminal trespass. Of course, the trespasser will probably give some lame excuse to the sheriff, who might buy it. But at least a record will be made, and that trespasser will leave your property alone in the future.)

Therefore, it is important that you construct a front gate near where your driveway joins the public road. The front gate need not be strong enough to hold back a car, just durable enough so that in order to open it when the gate is locked, some effort will be required and something broken. While that is possible, it rarely happens. Trespassers are lazy, and they usually won't want to hassle with a locked gate.

A lot of the country hardware stores sell front gate kits, and they might work. For my property, I built a front gate that is more durable, and this is what I advise.

To build such a front gate, you need to devote at least half a day, and buy the following items from a hardware store that caters to country properties: some good work gloves (costing about $5), a six-foot long, 20-pound digging bar (which costs about $35), a used railroad tie of six to eight feet long (usually $20), a 1-foot long three-quarters inch drill bit ($30 on up), a galvanized steel farm gate or tube gate of at least ten feet wide (up to $400), two or three bolt hooks, each long enough to get through nine inches of railroad tie (about $19 each), an eight-foot-long pressure-treated pole with a diameter of about four to five inches (about $15), a padlock and chain. It also might be a good idea to buy a few angry "No Trespassing" and "Beware of Dog" signs, and some flat-head roofing nails to hold the signs in place.

Bring along a three-foot level, a portable generator and power drill. Or you can buy from Home Depot a brand of portable drills under the brand name of Ryobi, which are adequate. The batteries that power them can be slowly charged up by a cigarette-lighter recharger, also sold at Home Depot.

The area where you will dig would ideally be rocky, or abundant with gravel. It is hard to dig there, but the railroad tie will stay put longer in rocky ground. Dig an outline of the railroad tie at least two feet below grade. After the hole is dug, and the railroad tie is inserted into it, use the level to hold the railroad tie up and use the digging bar to cram some rocks and dirt into the opening around the tie. Some people prefer to prop the tie up and pour some wet concrete in the hole, but I don't think this holds the tie in place as long.

There is an easier way to do this, but I don't think it produces as durable a front gate. Instead of a railroad tie, you can buy a treated fence post of at last five inches diameter and use an auger to dig the hole. The fence post will probably need some lateral support, or else in time, it will "lean" towards the farm gate, which will make opening and closing the gate a real hassle. You generally don't have that problem with railroad ties.

Once you have the railroad tie in the ground, and sturdy, hold the far gate up to the tie and determine where you want the holes to go in to support the farm gate. Make sure that the farm gate will swing open at least several inches above the ground, both in the open and closed positions. It is a good idea to make the farm gate even higher than you need. Use your drill to drill the holes through the railroad tie to support the gate. The bottom bolt hook will hold the gate up, while the top one will hold the gate in place. You can add a third one to take some strain off the bottom bolt tie. These gate hinges can be attached to the bolt hooks first, and then you can hold up the gate to attach to them, kind of like attaching door hinges to a doorsill and then attaching the door to the hinges.

Then you should dig a hole for the pressure-treated pole at the other end of the gate, where you want your gate to be stopped in its closed position. This post will also block the gate from swinging open on the other side.

When you have a hole of at least two feet below grade, hold the post there and cram a bunch of rocks and dirt into the hole with your digging bar, just like you did with the railroad tie. When you have that post in place, you can close the gate and wrap the chain around it and the post, then use the padlock to lock the gate shut.

You can now nail onto the railroad tie the "No Trespassing" and "Beware of Dog" signs. I like the "Beware of Dog" sign because while a trespasser can be warned about wrongly going onto your property by a "No Trespassing" sign, they will take notice if they are informed that they could be physically harmed if they trespass. A "Beware of Dog" sign changes things. I only wish I could add a counterfeit yellow sign from the local health department, saying "Rabies Quarantine Zone," so that the potential trespasser would worry that if they enter the property, they might be attacked by a rabid pit bull there!

Oh sure, this approach with these signs might be a little sadistic. But remember that we are talking about trespassers, who look to steal from you or raise your taxes, so the normal rules of human civility can be put on hold.

There is one thing that I have seen that makes it easier for you to open and close your gate, and I would like to mention it here. Assuming your driveway at this location is level, you could also buy a wheel to clamp onto the end of the gate that is opposite from the hinge area. That will also support the gate on the "unhinged" end and keep it from ever sagging.

You can also plant into the ground another pressure-treated post to hold your gate open when you drive through. However, it might just be easier to prop open the gate there with a large rock.

If you are like me, you will eventually get tired of driving to the gate, getting out of your car, opening the gate and propping it open, driving through, stopping your car on the other side of the gate, closing the gate, and then repeating all this when you leave your property. I began looking for an electrical gate system, and I found a great brand in Mighty Mule.

I won't go into the details of the Mighty Mule gate opener system, but I can say that I have been extremely impressed. I hooked up a control panel on my railroad tie, connected to a mechanical arm that opened and closed the gate by remote control. Up the hill from the control panel, I set up a Mighty Mule solar panel that was wired to the battery inside the control panel, keeping the battery fully charged. I even set up a metal detector in the ground, so that the gate automatically opens when I drive out of the property.

Might Mule has some great YouTube videos that show how to install all their parts, and the customer support is pretty good. Tractor Supply stores sell Mighty Mule systems, as does Amazon. If you invite others onto your property, you can set up a Mighty Mule numeric keypad outside your gate so that the gate can be operated by pressing a gate code on the keypad (you should also give the gate codes to the local police and fire departments). The whole set-up looks pretty cool and costs less than $400.

But keep in mind that a front gate is extremely important for your survival retreat. It is so important that you may want to time things so that you begin work on your front gate immediately after you have the driveway in place.

Chapter 10
Bug-Out Stuff

In the Afterword of my fictional book on electro-magnetic pulse, entitled *EMP: The End Of The Grid As We Know It*, I offered some advice on how to prepare to survive an EMP. I advised the reader to go on a camping trip. "I'm serious," I wrote, in case anyone thought I was joking.

I have seen some good books out there that have lists of what should be kept on hand to survive a societal collapse, but in my opinion, a good camping trip will provide you with the knowledge of what you will need in case of societal collapse.

Of course, the basics needed to survive on your retreat property are food, water, shelter, security, first aid, and sanitation. But a good sink-or-swim episode will leave the best impression on what you will need to survive on your own.

For that I will leave it to my friend Paul, who provided me with a first-hand account of surviving a possible tsunami on the Nicaraguan coast, and what he learned from it:

> Cal, just a quick note to impress on your readers the importance of being prepared with a bug-out bag, or something like it.
>
> Until now I have never been much of a prepper. I was raised in both Florida and the mid-west. If a storm or hurricane were on its way, we always had plenty of notice, sometimes days. I never felt the need have items

ready to go at a moment's notice. That all changed a couple months ago.

For the past six months, my wife and I have been managing a small B&B on the Pacific coast of Nicaragua. The area I am in is very difficult to get to, and only the most adventurous of travelers make it to our beach. At around 10 pm one evening we awoke in our hammocks to a very strange noise off in the distance. We couldn't for the life of us figure out what we were hearing.

Our neighbors knew what is was though, and they wasted no time at all. While we were still wiping the sleep out of our eyes, our neighbors quickly got their pick-up trucks loaded down with supplies and other neighbors.

They must have seen us looking at them quizzically, because one of them jumped off the back of the truck, and started yelling at us to hurry up and get on the back of the truck with them. Scared to death, and trying to translate his frantic Spanish, we jumped on board, and the truck then raced up into the hills at speeds that threatened to throw us off the back bumper. Every couple of minutes the driver would stop and pick up another family, most of whom were carrying five-gallon buckets.

Once safely in the hills, we finally got the story. There had been a fairly sizable earthquake off the coast, and we had totally slept through it. The sound we heard off in the distance was the tsunami warning sirens blaring in the nearest town about eight kilometers away.

We were completely and totally unprepared for this. I was wearing nothing but my swim trunks, and my wife wore her nightgown. Neither of us had shoes, drinking water, or even a flashlight. The locals just shook their heads and chuckled at our situation. They have had to do this before. Most of them lived through a tsunami in the 90's and lost everything. They have been through numerous earthquakes and tsunami warnings since then. There was no way they were going to be caught unprepared anymore. Luckily for us, Nicaraguans are extremely friendly, and they made sure to take care of us.

We were told that we would all be sleeping in the hills that night since the many aftershocks could also trigger a tsunami. The locals began unpacking their five-gallon buckets, which had been pre-packed for just such an occasion.

Out of five-gallon buckets came; canned goods, soup cups, bottled water, hammocks, bottles of rum, matches, and flashlights. Everyone there seemed to have a job to do. The kids took the flashlights and searched for kindling. The older kids went out with machetes to take some larger trees down. The women began the fires, while the men were getting the hammocks up. Luckily one of the families had an extra hammock for us, or else my wife and I would have been in the dirt with the bugs that evening.

While no tsunami hit that evening, it was quite a wake-up call for us. We spent that evening with a group of people who were overly prepared, and willing to help those of us who weren't. I doubt we would ever get that lucky again. Now, sitting by my front door at all times is my machete, and my five-gallon bucket full of bottled water, flashlights, matches, a first aid kit, our small roll-up hammocks, and enough food to get us through a couple of days. I won't get caught unprepared again.

Paul B.
Playa Maderas, Nicaragua

Chapter 11
Cars, Buses, RVs and Trailers

In my law practice, I used to appear in front of a judge who was mostly friendly, but very long-winded with his personal stories that he told to attorneys in chambers. When we attorneys would meet with this judge in his office to discuss our clients' cases, he would tell a lot of the same stories, over and over. And over.

One story that I heard several times was how this judge lived in his van while going to law school. The story was usually prompted by one of the attorneys in the room, within earshot, complaining to others nearby how much college tuition the attorney was paying for the attorney's kid. Following the complaint, the attorney would describe how the situation was remedied, like getting a loan.

"Oh, I got that one beat," the judge, after overhearing the complaining, would begin. "When I was in law school, I didn't have parents footing the bill for everything. After I had found out how much I would have to pay for housing, I decided to cut my costs, and I spent two years of my life living in my van, parked on the street outside."

In unison, half the room-full of lawyers would say "No way!" while the other half would start with "Van-down-by-the-river" Chris Farley imitations.

But hey, the judge did it! And you know what? I have driven by that law school several times since hearing that story, and I have noticed several current students doing the same thing. Bottom line: it can be done. If those law students can do it, and if that judge could do it, so can you.

Before I leave the topic of building a house on your property, let me tell you that there are some very impressive "kit homes" for sale out there. These are sold and delivered directly to the land-owner, meant to be assembled by the landowner with only a few tools. I have also come across a log cabin seller, Conestoga (at conestogalogcabins.com), that sells log cabin kits that are very impressive.

And it is always true, as I wrote in an earlier chapter of this book, that you should keep in mind what Bob Hope would do: have a long-term plan for your survival retreat that might include selling it if your needs change, or if local land values skyrocket.

So, if you do decide to build a house, it is okay to start with a small one. Should you ever put the property up for sale, it will be that much more attractive to a rich person, who will want to live in your little house while supervising the construction of a mansion elsewhere on the property. So there's that.

But if you want to set up a dwelling on your survival retreat -- both fast and cheap -- the absolute best option is to buy a car, bus, RV motor home, trailer, or a van, and use it as a dwelling. To take a couple of quick, random examples of what is available on EBay, I just found a 31-foot motor home with a "buy it now" price of $6,000, and a 16-foot RV trailer that sleeps three people, with a "buy it now" price of $5,000. Neither of these is something that I would necessarily want to be seen in or nearby, and transporting these RVs might be tricky, but they would provide a quick shelter at a survival retreat. I am sure that these deals will be long gone by the time you read this book, but these are just examples of what you can find.

Used school buses are especially inexpensive, no doubt because there are very few people who want to buy one. Running or not, it is possible to buy a used, full-size school bus for less than $5,000.

Once the seats are removed, the area behind the driver's area in a full-size school bus is approximately 280 square feet inside (8 feet wide by 35 feet long). Using a camping cot that is 75 inches long by 25 inches wide, it is possible to squeeze up to 15 cots inside. With an average inside height of 6 feet, bunk bed cots are possible, and that would double the occupancy. Not very comfortable, but still.

Some states require a special driver's license, just below a trucker's license, to legally drive a bus on a public road. So, buying a school bus might necessitate hiring someone with the right driver's license to deliver it, or upgrading your own driver's license.

It is also possible to build some pretty cool living rooms, kitchenettes, and bedrooms inside buses. This is loosely called a "bus conversion project." To see how it's done, check out some interesting websites I found, like vonslatt.com, hankboughtabus.com, and skoolie.net.

During the same EBay search I did for the motor home, above, I found a non-running RV van, similar to what Uncle Rico lived in in the movie *Napoleon Dynamite*, for a "buy it now" price of $850 and a step-van that was once used by Fedex, with enough room inside for several cots, for a firm price of $8,000. The Uncle Rico-type van I found is similar to what I had seen nearby that law school, and probably like what my judge friend lived in when he went to law school.

There are some regulatory considerations to remember: first, a trailer or a motor home that you plan on living in on your property should be registered with your state's department of motor vehicles as a "non-operating" vehicle. That way, you will pay very little to keep the vehicle registered. It might also be possible to end the registration of the vehicle altogether, saving some money.

Secondly, many states have a limit of how many vehicles, especially motorized vehicles, can be kept on a single parcel of land. It would be best to find out if and what the limit is at your property's jurisdiction, and stay within it. Thanks to satellite surveillance, the local government could find out if you have more vehicles than allowed on your property and pay you a visit.

You should also check the chapter on animals, later in this book, to acquaint yourself with what could be a big problem with any dwelling or vehicle on your property: mice and rats. Make sure that any dwelling or vehicle on your property is sealed tight from mice and rats, or else you will be in a constant war with them.

And take some advice from someone who has spent a lot of time in RVs: before attempting to live in, or spend any time in an RV, you will be more able to keep your sanity if you lower your expectations. You read that right: *lower* your expectations. See, RV's are cheap and tend to fall apart. If you keep that in mind from the beginning, you will be okay, and your nerves will be mostly intact.

To make things worse, most RV business repair places are pretty bad. During my first RV trip, I noticed that there is usually a hotel nearby an RV repair place. Why is that? Well, when people need repairs in their RVs, they check them in with the RV repair place, where the owner is promised a date and time for the completed repair. The anticipated completion date gets extended further and further away, and eventually, the RV owners spend a lot of time living in a hotel. Come to think of it, rental car companies could make a lot of money by having a lot of rental cars nearby RV repair places. The RV owners will need to have some way to get around, and they certainly won't be doing that anytime soon with their own RVs.

I once heard a podcast in which author Kevin Tumlinson complained that every time he and his wife used their RV, something new would break. Sometimes what broke was a decorative thing, like the trim on a book shelf. Other times an important thing, like the windshield wipers, would stop working. But it never failed: every single time he and his wife used their RV, something new would break. Without exception!

There are some great YouTube channels, like Bertha TV, Carolyn's RV Life, RVerTV, and The Wandering Wyatts, that document a family or someone's decision to sell their house and move permanently into an RV. While most episodes spotlight the different aspects of RV living, at least one or more episode will concentrate on something breaking down, and the RV repair place they limp to is either way-overpriced or not able to help at all.

As cynical as my previous few paragraphs may be, they make it a lot easier to resist the temptation to buy a shiny, brand new RV on a very high payment plan (or mortgage). If you ever find yourself inside one of these castles on wheels, whether it is an RV trailer or motor home, being pitched by a slick salesman, it is easier to fight the temptation to buy the RV when you realize most everything inside the RV will break apart and cause frustration. Just picture the RV as what it will be in a few years, and you will not want to pay a lot of money for it.

Here's another thing about RVs, and this may just be me: when our family began RV camping, it was amazing to me how many times I bumped my head. Seriously! Going from one part of the RV to another was quite a treacherous journey, usually involving a few head bumps along the way. It got so bad on one trip that I finally decided that when I needed to go to the restroom, it would be less painful just to leave the RV and find a tree nearby. The door out of the RV was closer than the RV's restroom.

So, by all means, if you plan on spending a lot of time living in an RV, lower your expectations. Don't get excited about RV living. They fall apart, and they can be uncomfortable. Once you have all that figured out, you will be fine.

And speaking of living in a really small vehicle, what about just getting a big, older car onto your property and sleeping inside it? A look through EBay or Craig's List reveals many huge cars with rotten gas mileage that are so big that they would be better used if they were just parked and slept inside.

But what's that like? I mean, could I really live in a car? For the answer to that question, I turned to an online friend, Rodney F., who had tons of advice:

Hi Cal,

I have some advice for the readers of your survival retreat book. I once had to spend a long period of time living in my car, including sleeping in it! I could see living in a car on a vacant piece of land, so maybe your readers can learn from my experience.

Throughout my life, I have had various disagreements with my parents about the way that they treated me, and because of my age, I made a few financial mistakes with little hope of paying for an apartment. It was no surprise that this was eventually the reason that I ended up living in my car for a while.

At first, I thought that living in my car would be horrible. To make things worse, winter was coming, and temperatures were dipping below freezing. But with some improvisation, I managed fine.

How did I keep warm at night?

To keep warm at night, I would sleep in my coat and ensure that any clothing underneath that was tucked into my trousers. If it got really cold, I would wear a sweater hat and wrap up my legs and feet with a blanket I got at a thrift store. I also used to (and this may or may not be advisable depending on your location) run the car's engine for minutes with the heater turned on. This worked out OK for me because it kept the car mildly heated and it charged the battery a little. But I have heard of others doing this, and the car exhaust would get inside the car, so that might be dangerous. It might be safer to do what I heard truckers do: they plug a portable heater into the cigarette lighter. But I did several things to prevent the chill from getting into my bones.

How did I keep cool during a hot day?

To keep cool during a hot day, I used to open all of the windows and drive around. This would give me the opportunity to wake up, and feel a little fresher. If I were stationary, I would open the trunk door (I had a hatchback). If I felt like staying put, I would let the engine run and turn on my car's AC for a while.

How did I sleep comfortably in the car?

Being rather tall, staying comfortable was tricky for me. But I tried all manner of things, including lying across the front seats and curling up on the back seat (which was mildly comfortable). But the most comfortable way of sleeping was by folding down the back seats and lying on both the back seats and trunk-hatchback area.

What about meals?

Living in a car comes with some difficulties, like eating meals. As I was struggling for money, I would wait until I was desperate and then I would visit a local store and stock up on essentials, like bottled water, dried fruit snacks, nuts, and bread. For the most part, this kept me going. When I had a little extra more money to spare, I would afford myself the luxury of ordering a takeaway (usually Indian or Chinese food) and have it delivered to my car. This would ensure that I was at least consuming something healthy. I found that surviving off of smaller meals helped me to come to terms with living in my car.

Protection from thieves

I parked my car in a quiet area where few people pass through, so the threat of thieves was minimal. However, there is always that small risk, so I decided that while I was sleeping in my car, every night I locked myself in the car with the key fob. That prevented anybody from quietly breaking open the doors or windows. If someone broke in, the alarm would go off, and with me being inside, I would be able to react quickly. Thankfully, I never experienced a break-in, but setting it up like this let me sleep better.

Another way I kept myself protected from thieves was to make as little noise as possible and keep to myself at all times. I figured that the quieter I was, the less chance there would be of my being noticed by anyone who might want to rob me. That was a good strategy the whole time I lived in my car.

Would I do anything differently if I had to live in my car again?

Definitely. I would have many more blankets, especially quilts and maybe even down comforters. I would also have more pillows to cushion my head from the hard parts of the trunk area.

I would also use a sun-shade for all the car windows. That way, at night the cold wouldn't come in as much, and during the daytime, I could better block the sunlight, which causes heat. Insulation.

Conclusion

Living in a car sounds horrible, and in reality isn't the greatest thing in the world. But look at it this way: you don't have to pay rent or other bills (other than fuel and insurance for the car), you could move it to wherever you need to move it, and you have all of your stuff with you. I found that my experience was what I made of it – I could have just crumbled and not made it through, but instead, I saw it as a blessing, as it gave me an opportunity to learn more about myself, regarding my resilience. It also helped me become more appreciative of the things I do have. Let's face it; there are plenty of people out there who have even less than someone who lives in a car.

--Rodney F.

Rodney's message had more to do with living in a car in a city, not on a property in the country. But I would agree with him that living in a car might not be that bad, and if you want to get something fast and cheap on your property in which you can live, a big car might be the best option.

Specifically, check out the Cadillac and Lincoln hardtop sedans, or their same-chassis counterparts made by Ford, Chevrolet, and the others, from the mid-1970's, or even the tacky station wagons from the late 1960's and early 1970's. All of these vehicles have appalling gas mileage, so they would be very inexpensive to buy on EBay. But they would be pretty good to sleep in. Remember, you aren't trying to make a fashion statement, you just want to have a quick and affordable dwelling on your survival retreat.

I must admit that the tone of Rodney's message caught me off-guard, as it was mildly-positive. If you look around online for stories of someone living in a car or van, you can find some mixed-to-positive reviews. There are a couple of great books out there, *How To Live In A Car, Van, or RV*, by Bob Wells, and *Walden On Wheels*, by Ken Ilgunas, which are very informative and positive. There are a couple of YouTube channels I found that chronicle living in cars, and they are pretty enjoyable: Hobo Ahle and Eileah Ohning.

An issue that Rodney touched on that I would like to mention here is the importance of blackout curtains, and not just for insulation. At nighttime, houses in the country that have lights on are easily seen by people far away, so you should cover your windows with blackout curtains. If you search for "blackout curtains" on Amazon, you can find some effective and even decorative blackout curtains for as little as $20 per window. I once bought something for $35 from Amazon called the Gro-Anywhere Blind, which is a blackout curtain with suction cups that is used for travel. This thing is excellent and fits on most windows. For the rare window that does not stick with the suction cups, just tape it onto the window with some duct tape.

One last issue I would like to cover regarding living in a car, bus, RV or trailer: camouflage. Remember what I wrote back in the chapter on Google Earth. A big school bus or RV will stick out on your property, if not to a snooping satellite overhead, then a hiker or a possible thief nearby, looking onto your property. If you do get a large vehicle with paint that makes it stand out on your survival retreat, do something about it. Cans of Rustoleum camouflage spray paint are available at Walmart for $4 per can. Granted, it would take a lot of cans of spray paint to make a big yellow school bus camouflage, for example, but it would be an important project.

Another option is to buy a huge ghillie net and drape it over your bus or RV, high enough so that you could walk underneath it even where the net extends beyond the roof of your vehicle-dwelling. You would need to fasten the net securely, and you should also drape it over several pressure-treated poles stuck at least two feet into the ground, with two-by-four boards nailed in to form an "x" at the top, so the ghillie net doesn't just fall through the pole.

Now that we are at the end of this chapter, I have an announcement: if you have followed the advice of this book so far, you now have a very basic and rudimentary survival retreat. Granted, your retreat will need some improvements, but you are now at a point where you have a start, and you will probably be able to stay alive and to keep your family alive in case of a truly SHTF-type situation.

So reach around and pat yourself on the back, but don't spend too much time congratulating yourself. Your survival retreat needs many improvements, and there are other issues you will need to know. The topics discussed in this book from here on will address needed improvements and other issues that are important for your survival retreat.

Chapter 12
Beware Of Thefts

If Dante were around today, writing a new edition of his book *Inferno*, I would suggest that he move the thieves to the lowest circle of Hell. I have been stolen from before, but after I had some stuff from my property stolen, I realized that there is no lower creature than someone who steals from another person's survival retreat. Not only do they take away some cool stuff that you paid for, but the thief violates the sense of privacy you have on your property. A place that has been trespassed upon and had stuff stolen from it just doesn't feel the same.

A property that is occupied only part of the time is especially vulnerable. If thieves know that you come to work on your property only on weekends or very rarely, they will show up when you are gone and take whatever they want.

I once had a couple of generators stolen, and when I reported the thefts to the local sheriff, I was asked to give the model and serial number of the stolen generators. Unfortunately, I didn't keep this information, but after tons of searching, I managed to find it on a charge slip. Still, although a report was taken, I was told that the chances of recovery were very slim. A trip to the local pawnshops and flea markets found nothing. (It is possible to deduct from your income taxes the value of stuff that has been stolen, but the amount has to exceed a certain percentage of your gross income. If you have had stuff stolen, look into whether you can deduct the value from your taxes.)

Since then, I take pictures of everything on my survival retreat that can be stolen. It's a whole lot easier than writing down serial and model numbers or trying to find a charge slip somewhere. For example, when I bought a replacement generator, I took several photos of the generator from several different angles, then I zoomed in and took a couple close-ups of the actual serial number. I have gone through several cell phones, and my photos always stay with me. I also attach the photos to e-mails and send them to myself and my wife. That way the model and serial numbers are kept safe in another location.

Having a lockable used shipping container on your survival retreat would also be a good idea. Those things are very secure and rugged. They come in 20 or 40-foot lengths, and every time I have been in the market for shipping containers, it seems I wind up looking at containers from a shipping port nearby, which makes sense. Often, companies around a shipping port will offer for sale their used containers, but also deliver them for a reasonable fee. A few years ago, I paid $2,500 for a shipping container, and $1,500 to have it delivered to my property.

But here is what to look for: after you decide what length you want, make sure you check out the container you are buying. Sometimes used shipping containers can get really beaten, and I have seen some with rusted holes in the walls or on the top. One container I saw came "pre-crushed" on one corner, so I gave it a pass. If you find a shipping container that you like, make sure you write down or photograph the numbers on the door, so that the container that gets delivered is the one you saw on the lot.

Also, I prefer containers that are colored green. I do my best to cover up my containers (*see* Chapter 4), but it is easier when the color helps the thing blend into the colors of your property. A container painted white would really stick out.

If you are tempted to try and cover up the container with dirt, make sure to fortify the top of it. Soil can extremely get heavy, especially after rain. And shipping containers were not designed to have such weights on the top, between the two walls. In time, the top of an improperly-buried container can sag and collect water, which would cause a lot of rust and shorten the usable life of the container. Even going inside a buried, the rusted up container would be unsafe.

And speaking of safety, and this is just my paranoia poking up its head, keep in mind that it is possible to be locked inside your container. Hypothetically, if you walk into your new container to marvel at the new storage space you have, the wind could blow shut the door, and the locking rods could fall into place. Sure, container doors and the rods that lock them are all very heavy, but still, a little paranoia with this issue is good. If I ever walk into a container alone, I make sure to prop open the door and keep my cell phone in my pocket, just in case.

Before having a shipping container delivered, make sure that the area where it will sit is good and flat, on top of the drainable soil (i.e., not solid clay soil), with several feet of open space all around it. It is possible to weld into place a "lock box" that will shield a special padlock that will fit inside and hold into place one of the locking rods. Check EBay for shipping container padlocks, which sell for about $30.

I recently saw a black "resin," 8 foot by 7 foot storage shed for sale at Costco for about $700. The thing felt rugged, and a sign on it claimed that it was steel-reinforced. There are also wooden sheds of similar sizes sold at Home Depot, for more money. My problem with buying them is that they would require a work crew on your property, checking things out and figuring if it would be worth a return trip, after hours, to steal something.

And this has to be a constant concern of the owner of a survival retreat. Any delivery that involves someone you don't know coming onto your property will include a chance that that person will figure the property is often uninhabited, ripe for stealing.

I always make sure that anything I order that needs delivery (like my backhoe) gets delivered to a trusted neighbor's property that is at least a mile away. Then, I drive the item to my property by myself.

And I am always on my guard about letting it get out that I am not on the property all the time. One time I showed up at my property and found a perfectly-balanced, empty beer can on the dirt road nearby my front gate. At first, I thought that someone had littered, but after thinking about it for a while, I concluded that someone nearby had carefully placed it there so that they could monitor my property. If that beer can remain untouched for a few weeks, I am convinced that someone would have concluded that my property was uninhabited and rarely visited by the owner. Then, thieves would have come onto my property, looking for stuff to steal.

Game cameras are getting perfected so that if you have a good cell phone signal or even wifi coverage on your property, you can buy camouflaged game cameras and hide several around your property. That way, if anyone comes onto your property, you will have several photos of them, their car and hopefully their license plate sent to your cell phone.

I'm pretty excited about one of the game cameras I bought for my property, and that is the subject of the next chapter. I'm almost looking forward to catching a thief with it!

Chapter 13
Game Cameras

As a land-owner, you should have at least one game camera on your land to watch out for animals. This will tell you whether your property has animals, like wildcats, that could pose a danger to anyone on your property, or whether there are animals on your property, like wild pigs, turkeys or deer, that you might want to hunt for food.

A game camera is typically about half the size of a shoebox, usually dark in color or camouflaged. It is powered by batteries and attached to a tree or pole to take pictures of anything that walks in front.

A problem I have had with my game camera is that in my quest to keep it as hidden as possible, I tied it to a tree that has some branches partially hanging in the way. In a typical month's worth of photographs taken by my game camera, about 90% are photographs of the nearby branches being blown by the wind into the view of the camera.

It's a trade-off because I want to keep this camera well-hidden, and I would prefer that it not be stolen by a trespasser who happens to walk nearby and see it. I could probably trim the branches back further, but the game camera would then be more visible from the road, and it could get stolen.

My game camera is a Bushnell, the same brand as the binoculars, and I am happy with it. The photos taken are in color and are very clear. About once a month I replace the SD camera chip inside it with a blank chip and examine the old chip on my laptop. I can bring up all the photos of the previous month by examining all the image thumbnails, which makes a scan of all these photos done very quickly.

I also have a Spartan GoCam game camera, which instantly broadcasts to my cell phone the photos or videos it takes of animals or whatever comes into view, and I installed this camera right near my front gate. That way I can get photos of the most thieving animals out there, those that have the scientific name of "homo sapiens cleptorous."

Whether you have the type of game camera that takes the photos and stores them on a camera chip, or a game camera that sends them straight to your cell phone, you should make sure to keep them well-hidden. The game cameras meant to photograph animals need not be as well-hidden because it is extremely rare when a deer has dismantled a game camera and walked off with it. But game cameras meant to photograph humans need to be extremely well-hidden. Metal boxes are also sold that make theft more difficult, but I believe they would make the photos taken less clear.

And despite the fact that the photos can be taken and instantly sent to your cell phone, after-dark photos are problematic, and a determined thief can return at night and steal your camera. Then, your best hope is to find it for sale at a local swap meet or pawn shop. (By the way, as with any expensive item you buy, make sure to take a photo of it, with the serial number clearly visible. That will increase the chances you can get it back if it ever gets stolen.)

The game cameras that send images to your cell phone are basically a separate cell phone with its own sim card and phone number, so you will need to activate it online, and you will pay a small monthly fee for this camera. Also, your survival retreat will need to have adequate cell phone coverage for such a camera to work.

Nowadays, Cabela's and Amazon charge about $100 to $150 for game cameras that keep the images on a camera chip. The cell phone-connected game cameras have just barely broken below the $500 mark. It's a pretty safe prediction that these prices will decrease.

Chapter 14

Animals: The Good, The Bad, And The Ugly

When I first moved from the city to the country, I noticed how I rarely looked down when I walked. In the city, that made sense. Other people you might come in contact with are about eye-level, and rarely was the pavement incomplete or dangerous. But in the country, if you keep looking eye-level when you walk, you could step on some animal or find your foot in a gopher hole, which would sprain your ankle, or worse. So I began looking down when I walked.

When you get your survival retreat, start looking down when you walk. You need to watch where you put your feet.

And yes, you will probably come across snakes. Whether they are poisonous or not, you need to make sure that you don't step on them.

I have a rule: poisonous snakes must go. No exceptions. Yes, I know, they get rid of mice or rats, and you just need to leave them alone, and they will leave you alone, blah, blah, blah. But look: if a poisonous snake is around me or a guest of mine, they might bite. So it must go. Simple as that. If you want to see something truly disgusting, do a Google image search of the term "rattlesnake bite," and just think: that could be you!

But how does someone kill a rattlesnake, water moccasin or other poisonous snake? I have shot several rattlesnakes with my guns, but I was never really convinced that they were dead.

Here is how you do it: first, have a round-head shovel handy, and begin by chopping the snake several times on its body. That will stop it from moving. Then, very carefully, press down and roll the shovel blade over the snake's neck over a hard surface, and cut off its head. Only when the head of a snake is separated can you be sure that the snake is officially dead. And keep in mind – and this is totally gross – that for a few minutes a detached snake head will still try to bite you. And its fangs still have venom.

In the past, I have put detached snake heads inside glass bottles and thrown them in the trash, but you never know if the bottle will shatter and someone will step on it, or whatever. The times when I have had an outdoor fire going, I have tossed the snake head into the fire and burned it to ash, and that satisfied me that the threat is gone.

Someday, I might cook and eat the rest of the rattlesnake I killed. I understand that the way to do it is to skin the snake and make sure the head, guts, and tail are gone. Chop the snake into sausage-size links, roll it in cornmeal or egg whites, sprinkle it with pepper, and fry in vegetable or olive oil. When you eat it, you have to watch out for the bones, but I hear it has a nice taste, kind of like dark-meat chicken.

But concerning the protection of you and your loved ones from poisonous snakes, I hope everyone is reading this book begins a new, life-long practice: whether you live in the country or any area where there might be snakes, you should have many round-head shovels everywhere around your house and property. Nearby your back door? There should be a round-head shovel leaning against the wall of your house, within quick reach. Same for all sides of your house. I also keep one leaning against the front of my house, but that's because I don't care if the shovel is something my guests see when they come to visit. If you value the non-cluttered appearance of your house, find a way to conceal your shovel, but have one nearby. You need to have a round-head shovel everywhere around your house.

Round-head shovels should always be on your mind as you shop at a hardware store. When they are on sale, pick up a few. Not only are they great to use in killing poisonous snakes, but they can also be used in, you know, digging.

Plastic bird netting is also a great snake killer. We mostly use plastic bird netting around our flower beds or planted vegetables to keep birds away, but it is amazing how this bird netting catches snakes. The snakes try to get through the netting, and they get hopelessly tangled up in it. Bird-X brand plastic bird netting (7 feet by 20 feet) can be bought on Amazon for $9, while Easy Gardener netting (3 feet by 50 feet) costs $8 on Amazon. I have seen both sold at Walmart, but it is seasonal there. If you don't find it in your local Walmart store, check its website or jet.com.

Plastic bird netting can be bought at much bigger sizes, but for the smaller sizes, I just drape it around the outskirts of a walkway. Every time I walk nearby, I check to see if any snakes have been caught in the netting. When they have been, I check to see if the snake is poisonous. If so, I pull out my round-head shovel and get to work.

Of course, not all snakes are poisonous and worthy of being killed. King snakes are black and white striped, and I have seen them eat mice and rats. Rumor has it that they also kill rattlesnakes. Gopher snakes are probably misnamed because they are way too small to eat gophers. Supposedly, they eat really small mice.

All snakes will surely startle you when you come across them, but if it is possible to safely move the non-poisonous snakes to remote parts of your property, you should. Once I caught two king snakes in some bird netting. I put on some leather work gloves and used some scissors to slowly cut back the plastic netting and free the snakes. Then, while holding the snakes by their necks, I drove them on my ATV to a remote part of my property. As I drove, the snakes wrapped their bodies around my arm, and this made the hair on the back of my neck stand straight up. I hate snakes. As I let the snakes go, I told them, "Y'all don't come back now, ya hear?"

You know, not all scary animals are dangerous. One time I saw some pretty obvious bear tracks on my property, and I promptly freaked. I rushed to my computer and researched local bears, and found that only black bears are known to be in my area, and black bears are reportedly more afraid of us humans than we are of them. That's pretty frightened! Since then, I have seen other bear tracks, so I know they are still around, but they have been avoiding me. Good!

If you live in a part of the country that has grizzly bears, watch out. I hear that they are aggressive to humans.

Mountain lions, also known as cougars, are very dangerous. If there is a mountain lion on or around your property, you and all of your pets and farm animals are in danger. They feed mostly at night and have big appetites. Their nighttime mating calls sound like women screaming.

Shotguns and pistols or at least .40 caliber would provide a good defense against mountain lions or other predatory animals. But here's a possible problem: depending on your area of the country, a mountain lion might be a legally-protected animal. If you get attacked by a mountain lion, and you kill it, you might find yourself the defendant in a criminal case, facing jail time and a huge fine. In such a situation, it may be best to "shoot, shovel and shut up."

I have come across foxes and bobcats, neither of which are very big or aggressive to humans. But if you have chickens or small pets, you need to protect them. I had a neighbor whose chicken coup was gotten into by a fox, and the fox killed every single chicken inside, then ate one of them. It didn't make sense, but whoever said foxes made sense?

Eagles and hawks can also be dangerous for chickens or small pets. For that reason, you should keep them inside a chicken coup or at least under the canopy of a tall tree.

We once had a mystery predator around our chicken coup, literally tearing our chickens up at night. One night I found that it was a raccoon, so it was quickly dispatched. It's weird how cute and cuddly some animal movies treat raccoons when in reality they are very cruel and despicable animals. Same for skunks.

In my opinion, armadillos are good and bad. If you find them on your property, keep your distance. They are more interested in digging holes all over, finding as many earthworms, grubs, ants and termites as they can. There is some evidence out there that handling armadillos or eating their meat can lead to leprosy.

For all these small animals, you will need a .22 caliber rifle to dispatch them. This size rifle and its ammo are the cheapest. The rifle is so cheap that it is easy to get a little extravagant. I once bought an AR-7, which can be disassembled and loaded into the stock, for only $250. What clinched the deal for me was that James Bond used this very gun in *From Russia With Love*.

Of course, not all animals are dangerous or bad. Some are good to have around. Owls are great at killing voles or other rodents that make a mess out of a typical farm. Owls like to make themselves at home in upper floors of barns or "owl boxes" that are on top of tall posts or high in trees. Owl boxes can be bought on EBay for $50.

Bats are also good to have around. They kill tons of mosquitos, and their poop makes great fertilizer. Bat boxes are smaller than owl boxes, and they must be placed on posts or buildings facing the sun. Bat boxes can be bought on EBay for about $20 to $50.

If you have a pond or any standing water on your property, consider getting some goldfish to add to the water. Standing water breeds a lot of mosquitos, but the mosquito larvae are very tasty to goldfish.

Earthworms are also beneficial. Occasionally I buy some earthworms meant to be used as bait for fishing and add them to my gardens. The worms till the soil and add air to the soil, making it easier for the roots of the plants to grow.

Before I finish discussing animals, I want to mention that on many areas on your survival retreat, you will find yourself at constant war with mice and rats. Anywhere on your property where their natural enemies have kept away, mice and rats will make themselves at home. First, you will find their poop everywhere; then you will notice paper towels and toilet paper shredded to be used for some nest somewhere, usually behind a fixture. Then you will notice that anything electrical that used to work will have brown-outs, or not work at all. That is because the mice and rats will have chewed through the electrical wires. Finally, you will notice a slightly-sweet but gross smell, indicating that mice and rats, their poop, and their dead bodies, are everywhere. It will be difficult to feel at home in such a structure, and you will have effectively lost the war on them.

For this reason, I advocate a pre-emptive attack on mice and rats, even before you see any signs of them. Place mouse and rat traps everywhere, whether it is the smashing type or poison. Anything that you can use and re-use to kill as many of them as possible.

I once felt bad for the rats I found and killed in an out-building, so I spent $60 on a "rat-zapper" rat trap, which would humanely electrocute any rat that came inside it. I figure that I killed three or four rats with this thing, at the same time that their cousins conceived and gave birth to about twenty-five other rats. After seeing how far I was behind in this war, I scrapped the rat-zapper and went for total destruction. It wasn't pretty, and my city-dwelling friends and relatives thought I was a mean and nasty animal-killer. But I knew the score, and how I needed to catch up if I hoped to reclaim this property.

Don't let this happen to you! You should begin fighting this war on mice and rats before you look around and realize you about to lose it.

Oh, and one other thing: if you spend any time on your survival retreat with your dog, you will find that they, and possibly you too, will pick up some fleas and ticks. Government officials are not the only type of parasites you will have to deal with on your property.

On my property, there is a certain area right near the creek where – it never fails – if my dog goes there, he will always come back with a tick or two.

Repelling fleas and ticks is usually expensive because the packages of flea and tick drops sold at grocery stores are expensive. My dog prefers the brands Frontline and Adventure, but these brands cost a lot. Hartz and Sentry are more affordable, but my dog doesn't like them.

It probably doesn't matter which brand you prefer, because in an SHTF situation the stores won't be open anyway. You will need to mix your own flea and tick repellant mix.

Here is a mixture I recently found on a prepper blog. The ingredients are cheap and easy to stockpile, and this mix works. In a spray bottle ($3 at Walmart), mix together one cup of water and two cups of distilled white vinegar (another $3 for a gallon at Walmart), with a couple spoon-fulls each of vegetable oil and lemon juice. Spray this on your dog's dry fur, or on your clothing and hair at least a couple times a day.

If you are too late, and a tick has embedded itself into your skin, get some tweezers and grab the tick as close to your skin as possible and gently pull it straight up until it lets go, then kill the tick in as cruel a fashion as you desire. Afterward, make sure to wash the area of skin, and your hands with soap and water.

If you don't have any tweezers or anything else to pull out the tick, go ahead and use your hand, but try your best not to squeeze the body so that the fluids from this creepy bug flow into your skin.

Here are some things not to do with embedded ticks: make sure you don't twist the tick as you pull it out because you might detach its head under your skin. And the treatment that seemed to work when I was a kid at summer camp, heating a tick with a match until it comes out on its own, is frowned upon by doctors and nurses nowadays. It seemed like yesterday when that method was strongly endorsed by our camp nurse, but I guess times change. Come to think of it, a few decades ago, medical doctors helped advertise cigarettes. Go figure.

Chapter 15
Flower Beds

I like dual-use things, and here is a good one.

If you have ever done any gardening, you will know that a raised flower bed is a great thing. With a raised flower bed, you no longer have to squat or lean over to allow you to water or weed your plants. You simply rest your fanny on the raised part of the flower bed and lean over a few inches to do your gardening.

What about this: instead of using wood or railroad ties, consider arranging the four walls of the raised flower bed with cinder blocks, and then filling them with rebar and concrete. Once the concrete is dried, these things are firm. You can then fill the bed with local topsoil and plant your garden as always. Moles and gophers would not be able to get into these raised beds, and it is easy to surround these raised beds with fencing material to keep deer away.

But here's the thing: in the event of a societal collapse or zombie apocalypse, if several of these raised concrete flower beds are arranged just right, you will have a structure to hide behind to defend the retreat. One could imagine the event where groups of marauders intrude and seek to take over, but the defenders will have something to hide behind.

It could make a difference.

Chapter 16
Food-Producing Trees

It would be a good idea to set aside some land on your survival retreat to grow vegetables in a location or method that will not be noticeable from people outside. The details of this are outside the scope of a book on getting and developing an inexpensive survival retreat, but I can refer you to a couple of great books on the subject: Rick Austin's *Secret Garden Of Survival* and Wayne Weiseman's *Integrated Forest Gardening*.

I have a longer-term idea I would like to present here: the planting of food-producing trees.

Let me start by saying that once you have your property, time will fly. You will look up one day, and realize that you have already had your property for five or more years. That is time that could have been spent passively growing some trees that will produce food to help you and your family survive.

Here is how to go about doing this. When you first get your survival retreat, familiarize yourself with the local climate and get to know what good food-producing trees will work in that area. Also, find out if there is a part of your property where the soil is moist. This might be an area nearby a stream or lake if one or both is on your property.

Then, dress up for hiking, bring along a three-foot long piece of rebar, and about ten to fifteen branches from existing trees or bare-root trees bought at a local nursery. That could mean apple, orange, plum, pear, avocado, or fig trees. Nut trees, like walnut, pecans, or almond trees, should also be considered. In some climates, blueberry or grape vines will work. Find a moist area of soil with decent but not overbearing sun, poke the ground with your rebar, and then plant the branch or bare-root tree in that hole. Then, forget about it for a few years.

At the same time, you should plant a cactus plant that will produce prickly pears. You will need to water this cactus until it gets settled. But once the cactus has grown a year or two, you can cut off some paddles from the cactus and plant them. In time, you will have started from a small cactus plant to several larger cacti, each producing prickly pears that you can eat.

Dryer, hot climates are also great for olive trees. There are several different varieties of olive trees, the best of which would be Frantoio, Kalamata, or Mission. In my opinion, producing good olive oil for cooking is important, hence the inclusion of Frantoio in this list, but the other two varieties produce large olives that can be cured and eaten.

Another great idea would be to plant Aloe vera plants. Like cactus, after they are planted, they need to be watered until they get established. The gel from Aloe leaves is great for burns, can be used as a skin moisturizer, even as a natural shaving gel. The gel from Aloe is antibacterial, so putting it on minor cuts will speed the healing.

But the point with this planting is to plant it and forget it, or at least give it minimal attention. Sure, some of what you plant will die, but in a few years, you may discover that some of what you planted have taken off in a big way.

Chapter 17
Heavy Equipment

It wasn't too long after we bought our property that we found we needed a contractor with a bulldozer to clear a driveway for us, and a contractor with a backhoe to spread some gravel and dig drainage ditches for us. While the need for dozer work was limited, the cost of the backhoe work was so high and continuing that I immediately developed an interest in getting my own backhoe.

Besides the issue of cost, I never knew whether these contractors had big mouths. How did I know whether they would alert their friends that there was a vacant piece of land that had on it some cool stuff to steal?

A couple of years later, I bought my own, used backhoe. Here are some numbers: when I hired a guy with a backhoe to come and work on my property, he charged me $80 per hour for two full days of work, or a total of $1,600. I paid $20,000 for my used backhoe, and in a few years, I had put 1,500 hours of work on it. That would have cost me $120,000 if I had hired the same backhoe operator to come by and use his backhoe. But during that timeframe, my only costs, besides buying the backhoe itself, was a new seatbelt, a break-check, a new owner's manual, and a bunch of diesel fuel. The savings was incredible, and working the backhoe is fun!

If I still had a need to clear more driveway, I would have also considered buying a used bulldozer. Fortunately, I found a local dozer operator who was very good and trustworthy. And while he was expensive, he was good and the jobs I needed him for were finite.

From time to time, there is a need to move a lot of gravel from where it is delivered, near the front gate, to further back into the property. I have never owned one, but I have repeatedly been tempted to buy a Bobcat.

When you buy any heavy equipment, the most important associated purchase is an owner's manual. Don't get cheap on that. An owner's manual teaches you how to safely operate your equipment, and it could save your life.

My backhoe owner's manual is amazing in how many times it cautions me that if I do a certain movement the wrong way, the result could lead to "serious injury or death." No sugar-coating there! This book immediately gave me a healthy fear of my backhoe.

If you hesitate in buying a piece of heavy equipment such as a backhoe, give this a try: rent one from the local heavy equipment rental place, and hire someone with some experience to operate it for you. Then, find and read the machine's owner's manual, and ask the operator to let you run it for a while. Make sure the operator knows that you are a rookie with this machine (with heavy equipment, it is a good idea to put aside all of your pride), and have them ready to take over. You should have a healthy fear of the machine, but you will probably like working it.

I have some quick safety tips: tell anyone on the ground nearby that they need to stay at least 25 feet away from the machine when you are operating it. On a backhoe, for example, the boom arm on the back can swing so quick that it can hit someone before you realize they are even there. Also, whether you are parking the machine or operating it on a hill, always assume the brakes will give out. When I park a piece of heavy equipment, I make sure it is on a level area, or I have the tires turned in such a way that the machine is secure, with or without the parking brake engaged. I don't want to worry about the machine running off downhill and driving over someone. Even when I am operating my backhoe, I have the front scoop ready to drop, at an angle, if the engine dies and the transmission disengages. That has never happened to me, but I believe it is possible, and I want to be ready. And finally, be extremely careful driving these machines on hilly terrain, because many are top-heavy and could easily fall over.

ATVs are also good to have on a survival retreat. Many times you will find that your equipment and supplies are far away from where you will be working on a project, so having a good ATV, and maybe even an ATV trailer, will help.

I found that EBay has great selection and prices for ATVs. Arranging for the delivery was tricky, but I used Forward Air and was satisfied.

As with heavy equipment, ATVs are fun but potentially dangerous. I once saw an injured man at a community center near my survival retreat. He had a broken nose, both black eyes, a broken arm, and a dislocated shoulder. The reason: he was driving an ATV that tipped over.

If you have to have more than one ATV on your property, it would be a good idea to have them the same make, model and year. That way, if need be, you can cannibalize the parts from one of the ATVs to keep the other one running.

Regarding thefts: believe it or not, it is possible to have one of these vehicles stolen. A neighbor or mine once had his dozer stolen.

Ideally, you will have a barn or some locked enclosure. But if you have to leave it out in the open, try to park it beneath some trees, with a cover over it. A tarp will have to do for a dozer or backhoe, but covers for ATVs are made for their exact measurements. If you can, you should also unhook some of the electrical wires or remove the battery.

Chapter 18
Cache Tubes

I have done a lot of writing in this book about the vulnerability of things on your property being stolen. Now I would like to write a little about something that will help you keep your stuff from being stolen.

Behold the cache tube. It is a modern-day treasure chest. The cache tube is a 2-foot long by 4-inch diameter black ABS pipe with a cap on one end and a plug on the other. There is enough space inside this tube to keep a small pistol, extra ammo, a lot of important medication, some food, tuna fish pouches, MRE's, Mountain House freeze-dried food pouches, extra clothes, leather work gloves, and a lot of silver coins that can be used for barter in case of societal collapse. It is possible to buy a tube with a wider diameter, but the costs for a wider cache tube go way up.

I recently went to Lowe's and spent about $50 for the parts to this cache tube, the ABS glue, plumber's tape, and a bunch of nuts and bolts. I recommend you have several of these cache tubes buried at different locations on your property. The plumber's tape will help keep this thing watertight if it is buried and rain cakes the ground.

Why the nuts and bolts? As long as you have anything buried on your property, including a cache tube, you should toss nuts and bolts all around. That way, if anyone with a metal detector shows up and tries to find anything buried, they will find so many of these nuts and bolts that they will get frustrated, give up and leave.

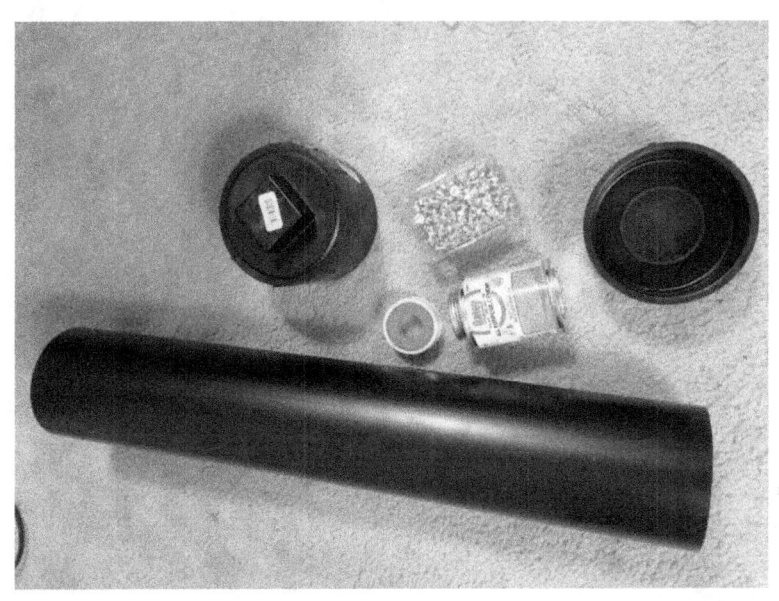

Chapter 19
Fire Issues

Remote properties in the country have a unique set of fire issues.

First, brush can grow out of control, and if the area has not had much rain lately and it has been hot for a while, there is a danger that the whole area could go up in flames.

In third world countries, this is not much of a problem. Fires are routinely set to cut back on the brush and out-of-control forestry. But in the United States, expensive homes built in the middle of forests are burned down, leading to insurance premium hikes, sometimes deaths, and so on.

This is why it is difficult to get insurance for your property that covers fire damages. A good rule of thumb with insurance is this: if you need a certain type of insurance, it is likely to be very expensive or impossible to get.

Of course, you can minimize the fire danger with any structure you build on your property, by making sure that there is a nice "fire break" around it. Fire needs flammable vegetation to spread, and if there is very little or no vegetation immediately around the buildings on your property, the fire danger is minimized. Whatever the local fire officials say is a good distance between vegetation and your buildings, you should increase it somewhat, to be extra safe. (This presents a trade-off, because with less vegetation around the structures on your property, the structures will be more visible to the public. This is why it is best to construct your buildings out of local stone, or in materials that are colored so as to blend in the with surrounding area.)

Weed-eaters are both a blessing and a curse. Every spring, a lot of land-owners dust off their weed-eaters and try to cut back on the brush while the brush still has some moisture in it. If this happens early in the springtime, the goal is met, and the brush is cut back and the fire danger is minimized. But it never fails: some people will try to use their weed-eaters in late spring or in early summer, and they actually cause fires by kicking up stones and causing sparks in dry areas. I remember when I first moved to the country and heard about several large regional fires that were caused by people using weed-eaters, in an attempt to cut back flammable weeds. You would think if they just let everything alone, there would be less a chance of a fire!

Another fire issue unique to remote properties in the country is the occasional trespasser who sets up a methamphetamine lab. It doesn't make too much sense, but then again using and/or selling meth doesn't make too much sense either. But every once in a while a fire will seemingly come out of nowhere, and when the smoke settles, firemen will find implements that were used to make meth. So keep a look out for remote areas of your property where that could be going on.

What to do with debris is another issue. As you clear parts of your survival retreat for hiking trails, driveways and living areas, or whatever, you will eventually find that you accumulate a lot of debris. All those tree branches and bushes that were once part of the area where you now drive will start to build up, and get in the way.

What do you do with all this debris? You cannot just leave it there and hope that it breaks down and composts. Sure, that may happen naturally, but it takes decades, not weeks to have dead bushes and tree branches become compost.

And taking this stuff to the local trash dump is expensive. Every time I have checked the local trash dump, the costs for dumping "yard waste" was very high. And that was assuming I could somehow get all this stuff into the back of my truck.

It is for these reasons that people in the country usually put all their debris in piles and just burn them. A few years ago, at my property, it was quite a relief to look at an area that used to be filled with dead bushes and tree branches, and see them all gone, replaced by a small pile of ash. Problem solved!

But be careful, and it is extremely important that you keep it legal. If you start a fire in a pile of dead bushes and branches, and the fire gets out of control and expands beyond your property, you may be billed to pay for the firemen who had to come and put it out. And if your fire expands to burn the whole area, well, you will have a number of lawsuits and worse to contend with.

I hope I have scared you about debris burning. Debris pile burning is useful but risky. Of all the scenarios discussed in this book about "ways to do it right" and "following the local rules," this is right up there at the top. Don't even be coy when you approach the local fire control officials and ask about burning rules. You and the fire control officials are on the same side. You both want to keep the debris burning under control. And besides, a fire is easily seen in the country, and people in a distant watchtower will be able to easily see that there is a fire on your property.

Let me tell you of my own experience with an out-of-control debris fire. I followed all the rules about time of year (springtime), size of debris pile, and distance of the fire from other vegetation. I even faxed an advance notice to the local fire control powers-that-be. Things were fine until a freak gust of wind blew the flames in an unexpected direction, and lit a nearby dead tree on fire. From there, the fire moved from bush to bush, up a nearby hill and threatened a dense forest I had never been in.

I called 911 and my down-wind neighbor, in that order. The firemen came within minutes. I remember that they casually asked me if I wanted the fire to go on a little, to create a future fire-break. Apparently, they were not as nervous as was I about this fire. Diplomatically, I asked them to put out the fire as soon as possible.

Then came a particularly nightmarish event: inmates from a local prison arrived to help put out the fire. Apparently, fire abatement is now a vocational-training program offered to some inmates. How nice! Don't get me wrong – I know there are a small percent of innocent people in prisons, but having a whole truckload of them on my property was quite astonishing. What if they noticed the route taken to get to my property, and one or more of them decided to pay me a visit once they got paroled? Needless to say, this was the opposite of "operational security."

In the end, what I felt would be The Fire Of The Century burned up less than one acre. And the "bill for reimbursement" that I was warned of never came, and I never reminded anyone.

So before you plan on burning any debris on your property, check with the local fire control government office, and follow the rules. Some "fire paranoia" might even be in order.

They will probably have a procedure whereby you file something in advance, and you need to follow the rules. For example, never start a fire, even a campfire, in an area that has not had any rain in a long time. Winter or early springtime, after a lot of rain, are the safest times of the year for fires. And always be nearby your fire. Never leaving it unattended, even when there are small flames. And make sure that your debris pile is smaller than a VW Beetle, far away from other vegetation. Keep at least a good 10-20 foot area around the pile.

Starting a debris fire soon after rain would be a good idea, and you should assume, like I didn't that day, that the wind *will not* cooperate. One thing I did right was that I left open the front gate, just in case a fire truck needed to get onto my property in a hurry.

And finally, when a fire is out, there may still be hot coals that could reignite. So, when you are done with the fire, do your best to make sure the coals are out.

In some areas, it is legal to have a "burn barrel," with is an old 55-gallon metal drum that has a small hole cut near the bottom. The oxygen is sucked into the hole at the bottom, and the contents of the barrel burn pretty quickly. The problem is that sometimes the sparks and embers that come up from the barrel are get blown downwind, threatening other areas. Whether you can use a burn barrel is another of the questions you should ask the local fire control office.

One last fire issue I want to mention here is the danger posed by parking a hot car on an area that has a lot of weeds. The exhaust pipe that runs along the bottom of a running car can be extremely hot. If the car is parked at a location with a lot of dry weeds, don't be surprised if a fire ignites and sets the car on fire. You should make sure to warn not only your family of this danger, but also any guests to your property, and members of your survival retreat group.

Chapter 20

Fencing

Once you have anything planted, the local animal population will thank you. Deer, raccoons, foxes, possums, skunks, moles, and many more animals will not be able to wait to get into your garden to eat what you have planted for them.

That is why it is very important to have secure fencing around your property, but at least around the areas where you have something planted.

The fence should be secure on the bottom so that animals won't be able to burrow under the fence. Deer are great at jumping over fences, and white-tailed deer can jump over a fence as high as eight feet. The height of your fence depends on the animals in your area.

You could hire a local fence-installing company, but you run into the problem of having people onto your property, noticing that there is usually no one home. The workers could decide to return later and help themselves to the stuff you have there, and they would also cost more than what you would spend doing it yourself.

If you choose to build your own fence, I would also advise fencing a smaller area so that you get some practice on putting up a fence. Once you know how to competently put up a small fence, you can tackle a larger area or even the outline of your whole property.

When I began my fencing operations, I went to the local farm supply store and picked the brains of the salesmen there. I found that the ingredients were: pressure-treated wooden posts, studded t-bar posts, a post driver, a 3-foot level, a length of fence, which I decided to use standard wire fence that is six feet high. I also needed wiring to tie the fence to the metal posts, and u-nails to nail the fence to the wooden posts. I decided not to use barbed wire, as it was not necessary. (It is possible to make some much more decorative fences, like wooden-outline fences or split-rail fences, but I decided to stick with the utilitarian, 6-foot tall wire fence.)

I decided to alternate the wooden and metal fence posts in the ground, about six to eight feet apart. The wooden posts provide most of the support for the fence, and the metal posts keep the fence from sagging. I had to dig at least a two-foot hole for each wooden fencepost.

There are many machines, called augers, that will enable you to dig a fence post hole. The best one by far that I have found is the Ground Hog HD 99. Seriously, this auger is great. After renting one from a hardware store, I bought a used one on EBay for $1600. The Honda engine and the hydraulic engine of this thing make digging a 2-foot post hole a breeze.

Another great thing about an easy-to-use auger is that, in case of a zombie apocalypse, it can help you incapacitate a dirt road to your property so that zombies will have a hard time getting there. (*See* Chapter 1.) I had the character in one of my dystopian books do that.

Whatever dimension of the fence you are building, you will need to leave a gap between two wooden posts the same length as a fence door that you will use to get in and out of the fenced-in area. This could be a farm gate, bought at the same store where you bought the farm gate used at the front of your property (*see* Chapter 9), except this one is only three feet wide. To make this fence door animal-proof, attach metal posts to the door and wire some fencing them. It won't look as pretty as the rest of the fence, but at least the fencing will be continuous.

Chapter 21
Tiny House

The "Tiny House" craze is sweeping the country. And, if you can handle living in a house that is extremely small, well, "tiny" (200 square feet), and have limited stuff there, it looks fine.

Nowadays, building a regular house can cost anywhere from $100 to $200 per square foot, so the main advantage of a tiny house is the low cost. Tiny houses rarely require permits, which is cool. Most of the time a tiny house is on wheels, so it is not considered a permanent structure. While a tiny house is driven on the public roads, it will need a license plate and obey the rules of other trailers. But once it is parked on a property, it can be registered as a "non-operating" trailer, and the state motor vehicle department fees will be very low or non-existent.

The plumbing in a tiny house can be tricky. It may be possible to get water into the tiny house without a permit, and sometimes "gray water" waste (non-sewage) can be dumped onto the ground to harmlessly leach into the soil.

As for sewage, or "black" waste, tiny houses usually have a composting toilet, and this can be a problem. Not all jurisdictions allow you to have a composting toilet on your property. And a lot of times they smell like sewage, which is a little off-putting.

Although a composting toilet might look normal, after the contents of the bowl are flushed, the waste goes to a composter, either immediately below the toilet or below the floor. The composter heats the waste with a solar panel or a small battery and then turns the waste to ash. Sun-Mar, Biolet and Envirolet are the main brands of composting toilets.

I have seen people on reality TV shows rave about their composting toilets. But I have also seen owners of composting toilets use the ash from the composter on their vegetable garden. While I am not a nutritionist or biologist, I am pretty sure this is a major no-no.

All that having been said, tiny houses are cheap, and I promised a book on putting together a survival retreat that is very cheap. So a tiny house is one alternative to consider.

Included below is a testimonial I got from a friend who loves her tiny house. Although she calls it a tiny house, I think it really is a shed because it is permanently part of the property. Whatever. The testimonial also covers some other issues, like off-grid power and composting toilets, subjects that are covered more in detail elsewhere in this book. I thought I would include this testimonial to help give you an "owner's perspective" of constructing and living in a tiny house.

Cal, feel free to include in your retreat property book my comments below, in which I outline my goal to live in an off-grid tiny house.

My tiny house, off the grid, has been quite an adventure!

I still don't feel qualified to give advice, but here is some: lesson one, start slowly and give yourself a realistic timeline. As an environmental scientist, I had met many people who lived off-grid to save money, save the environment, be more self-reliant, be prepared for disaster or just because they truly enjoyed the survivalist lifestyle. Since I already lived in a small house, they frequently suggested I go off-grid and get in touch with nature. Since

I thought it would be easy, and I had two months' vacation coming up, I thought I would do it. I was ready to prove that I was just as tough as they were. I had only two weeks to get ready; that was my first mistake.

Fortunately, I did not have to worry about buying land. I have a plot several miles from the city surrounded by wilderness. I knew the plot like the back of my hand because I frequently hiked through it, harvesting herbs and wild berries as I went. As I set about planning my tiny off-grid house of only 200 square feet, I considered all the possible building materials. Why buy costly insulations when I could use straw bales? Why cut a pine when I could use fast growing more renewable wood sources such as bamboo? Then I thought about using rammed earth, papercrete, and even hempcrete. Filled with passion, I could already see it completed with solar panels, tubs for rain collection, an inside toilet with piping to an exterior composting system with gravel filtration, and an adorable loft to add space for storage. I began thinking about living in this home permanently, not just during vacations.

Then I started pricing things, and reality hit. My best bet was to look for naturally occurring and free resources. The soil around me was sandy loam, so making adobe bricks was not going to happen. Similarly, with the high humidity papercrete and hempcrete were also not good options. Seeing a construction site, I noticed a great deal of trash that was perfectly usable including old growth hardwoods, wide knot-free planks, doorknobs, tile, plumbing fixtures, and even furniture. I decided to go traditional with a wood frame, but use straw bales for insulation. Everything went easily and, with help from some friends, I was able to finish the basic construction in a weekend, not the one day I had planned, but still not too far behind schedule. I had my tank on the side of the house for collecting rain water and a large bucket, with a hole cut and tubing leading to my compost bed, for sewage. Yes, I planned to garden, so had built a compost bed while we were building the house. It was a simple two-stage system. By Monday, it was already filled with some of the food scraps from meals the building group and I had over the weekend. I know many of my friends had no electricity in their homes. They relied on wood for heat and cooking. Candles provide them light. I figured that I could do that too.

After spending one very cold night trying this, I had my next project, electrification. I could adapt to a bucket toilet. I could use colloidal silver that kills pathogens in collected rainwater and stream water to use for drinking and bathing. I could use buckets and a basin, which was tubed to my garden area, for bathing. I could not adapt to the heat from fires during the warm summer days. Within a day, I felt myself getting seasonal affective disorder from only having candlelight from around 7 PM until 7 AM. I needed electricity, if for no other reason than to prevent a mood disorder! The price of this almost stopped my heart. I had not even spent $50, including buying food for friends who helped me build, in constructing the house. However, a small wind turbine and the associated equipment would cost over $5,000 for just a few kilowatts. Additionally, there were times the wind in the area was in the wrong direction, so this would be worthless. Furthermore, due to the height of the tower needed, there were more permits required than I care to think about. As an environmentalist, who has worked with airports on bird issues, I was also a bit afraid of harming birds. Now the second option was a solar system with a self-contained battery bank. I was a bit worried about the toxins in batteries, but I could get a kit for a few hundred dollars. After calculating my usage at around 70 watts, I chose the Grape Solar 100 watt kit. This gave me some safety during cloudy days. Many of my friends laughed when I got such a small system, but all I needed was electricity to keep an emergency phone charged and lighting a few hours a day. Now, those who consider doing this should remember to buy mounting brackets, surprisingly, these did not come with the kit.

During these first months, I met some others and had fun bartering. I do not think I spent a dime, other than in construction, the entire time. It was very liberating. Now, I do enjoy medical insurance and some modern luxuries, so I did not choose to continue to live entirely off the grid. I have since upgraded to a larger solar system so that I can use the computer. I now have Internet connections in the home. In fact, that is how I am writing and delivering this piece to you. However, I did decide to stay in my no-running-water, solar powered, and freeing tiny house. I commute to work but spend my evenings and weekends off-grid, even renting out my small house in the city.

The biggest lesson I learned so far is to start slow and give yourself time to learn and adapt. If I had it to do over again, I probably would have no loft, no fireplace, and a more functional home. I also would have angled my roof more to help maximize collection of rainwater. However, by trying to do everything at once, I didn't give myself time to experience or fully research off-grid living before construction. If I had, I might have considered a micro-hydro system to feed the solar battery bank. Although that would have lengthened my construction time, especially since there might have been even more permit requirements. Also, I have a few regrets in how I designed my home; but hey, I love living in my off-grid, tiny house! I cannot imagine ever going back!

--Alicia M.

Chapter 22

Decoy House

You're about to read something that is very rare. No, not the "decoy house" idea, although that is also pretty rare. I'm talking about a prepper author who actually admits that what he is about to write of is a little strange. Usually, I'm a pretty normal person, but don't we all have a strange side, filled with strange thoughts? I know I do. And I have good company: Jim Morrison and The Doors had a hit song, "When You're Strange," that celebrated all things strange. I think I'll make that my theme song.

And, full disclosure, I have never done what I am about to suggest. But I would love to.

I'm talking about a non-essential (but fun) thing: a "decoy house," just inside the front gate of your survival retreat.

Here's the idea: you have a property way out in the country, not surrounded by much, and a front gate and driveway that join the local county road. Just inside your front gate, you build a "fake" house that looks like it is lived in. It can look like a standard three-bedroom, two-bathroom house, with doors locked and window-shades drawn, but otherwise looks like people live there. With some power hook-ups and electrical timers hooked up to lamps and radios inside the house, you can make it so that at certain times of the day or night, lights and/or music will go on in this house. That way, passers-by or even trespassers will believe that this house is the main one associated with your property, occupied.

Bill collectors, traveling salesmen, stalkers, process servers looking to ambush you, basically anyone who would like to invade the sense of privacy you have on your country property, with whom you would rather not come in contact, would be distracted and frustrated by your decoy house.

The possibilities are endless, but here are a few ideas that will help you have a more convincing decoy house:

Install a doorbell that is hooked up to a recording that announces you are home but sick or otherwise unable to answer the door, so the visitor is asked to come back later or leave any deliveries at the front door. Ferris Bueller did this on his day off.

With "smart house" technology, you could install video cameras, microphones and speakers that enable you to view or interact with people in the front of, or anywhere around, your decoy house, and make them think you are just inside, wanting to be left alone. This would require an Internet hook-up there, which is a hassle, but you would be able to access the cameras from your cell phone far away.

Leave a couple of half-full trashcans outside the decoy house. Sometimes stalkers or trespassers will look inside trashcans to get an idea if anyone really lives in the house. With at least some trash in those trashcans, they will believe you live there. Just make sure that the trash you put there is not dated, like a telephone bill from years earlier.

Keep up some minimal landscaping at the decoy house. Overgrown weeds or plants will give it away that no one really lives there.

Park and lock a late-model car nearby the front door. I'll even award you some extra points for leaving a package of chewing gum or potato chips on the dashboard, in plain sight. This will make it look as if the car has recently been driven. And make sure to start the car and move it a few feet back and forth every few weeks, not only to keep the battery charged, but also to make sure that weeds or leaves don't collect around the tires.

Keep in mind that the truly determined stalkers or trespassers will check Google Earth (*see* Chapter 4) and make sure that this house really is a house and not just an empty façade. Therefore, consider having what looks like a real roof. And while you are at it, make your real house, further up the driveway, *not* so visible on Google Earth.

Another good idea would be to have a second electric gate that blocks the driveway that goes further up into your property to your real house. Ideally, you could attach to this electronic gate a bunch of dried leaves or debris, so that anyone who is there and looks at it cannot see that it is a real gate, as opposed to a pile of debris.

Here is a caveat: as with all advice in this book on what to do with your property, I encourage you to follow all permit requirements for your area. In some strict jurisdictions, this might make a "decoy house" impossible.

But the main objective with a "decoy house" is to distract anyone who would violate the sense of privacy you have in your real house, and occupy them and waste their time at the front door of your decoy house.

Chapter 23

Off-Grid Energy

This is a book about acquiring a survival retreat, and it includes some chapters on issues that are relevant to a reader who wants to acquire such a property. Therefore, what follows is an introduction to off-grid energy components and systems. And I promise to keep this complicated subject relatively simple.

First, keep in mind that as you learn more about the terminology, science, and components of off-grid energy systems, it will be very easy to get intimidated and frustrated. The science can be challenging, and it will take some time to get to know the purpose of all the components. My advice is to keep reminding yourself that this stuff is not impossible to learn and that eventually, the knowledge of all this will sink in. Try your best to stay positive! If all else fails, try to find an explanation of off-grid power from a person of limited intelligence, either in person or on a YouTube video. That way, you can figure that if someone *that* stupid can figure all this out, then, by golly, so can you!

And not all off-grid power systems are that complicated. I once visited a friend of mine at his "palapa" on the beach in Mexico. He lived in a big tent, with rechargeable battery-powered lanterns, some cots and a makeshift kitchen that had propane-powered burners and ovens. He also had a propane-powered refrigerator/freezer. For power, he had a couple of solar panels hooked up straight to a car battery. When he felt the need to take a shower, he would fill up a plastic basin with fresh water, connect a submersible water heater to the car battery and heat up the water. He would then connect a dismantled RV shower system to the car battery, and take a warm shower. Whenever the clouds would block the sun for long periods of time, he would pull out a Honda 2-kilowatt gasoline generator and charge the battery for a while.

He played it all by ear. Overcharging the battery, or keeping the charge low so that the battery's life is shortened? He didn't worry about it. Safe ventilation around the battery? The sea breezes around made it safe enough. It was a very simple, off-grid power system.

But charging a car battery without keeping track of how much it is charged could be dangerous. Batteries can discharge corrosive gases that will create rust on tools or other metal things nearby. Even scarier, under the right conditions the fumes emitted from a battery can cause an explosion. I had a great time visiting my friend at his place in Mexico, but the more I learn about off-grid power, the more I shudder when I remember the chances we took with that car battery.

My friend should probably have gotten himself a Yeti, sold by the company Goal Zero. A Yeti is a similar set-up -- basically a car battery -- which is 12 volts of DC electrical power, able to be charged by a solar panel or even plugged into a wall charger to charge it up. It is inside a sturdy plastic box with an inverter that allows you to plug into it AC electrical appliances, USB computer or cell phones. The Yeti also tells you when its battery is low, so when needed you can charge it back up. It is a handy little thing, but Yetis cost a lot of money: $400 up to $2000, depending on which bells and whistles you want to have. I have seen the Yeti for sale at Emergency Essentials, Amazon, Lowe's, Costco, and Home Depot.

Oops! I'm already talking about complicated power issues! You know, DC and AC power. Sorry.

Maybe I can back up and explain the terms DC and AC power. When electricity is generated and stored in a battery, it is DC, or "direct current," power. Your car is one big DC power system because the power is generated by the car's alternator and then stored by the car's battery, then used in the spark plugs, lights, instruments, air conditioning, and butt-warmer.

DC power is good electricity, except it does not travel well. The DC power that begins in a copper electrical wire is not the same DC power that comes out the other end. More than a few feet of transmitting DC power can be very energy-costly. As a historical matter, Thomas Edison envisioned DC power powering whole neighborhoods until he noticed that the large loss of DC power across long distances.

AC, or "alternating current" electricity, travels much better. As electricity was first developed in the olden days, it was discovered that AC power could be transformed, meaning the voltage greatly increased, and it would travel extremely well. Then, the AC power arrived at a house where it would be used, so a transformer was set up nearby to lower the voltage for use in the house.

But AC power is not storable in batteries. To use electricity from a set of batteries in a house, the batteries must first be hooked up to an "inverter," which changes the electricity from DC to AC electricity. Inverters are used everywhere that DC and AC power needs to be converted. That bulky box that is part of your laptop charger? It's an inverter.

Batteries and inverters are the heart of all off-grid power systems. Before setting up an electrical system, you should have an idea how much power you will need, and buy batteries and inverters that will supply the needed power.

Now let me mention the tax and government subsidies that enter into the picture. I have a few friends who own homes in residential areas, and they have many solar panels on their roofs. They have what are known as "grid-tie" systems because their houses are still hooked up to the local electrical grid. The DC energy generated by the solar panels is converted by an inverter in the house and then hooked up to the grid, enabling the home owner to "sell (AC) power" back to the electricity company.

For a lot of homes, this is fine. The subsidies and tax advantages to doing stuff like this are nice, and it is cool if you can cut your power bill to almost nothing while paying a tax-deductible payment plan on the solar panels and inverter that were bought. And the homeowner can brag about it all to people at a farmer's market or PTA meeting.

However, keep in mind that if you are interested in cutting the umbilical cord to the power grid and having an off-grid power system, you will generally not get any tax deductions or government subsidies. Electrical contractors will also try and convince you to set up a grid-tied electrical system. For the contractor, it is a lot easier to get paid when there is a pot of golden subsidies and tax credits in the mix.

If you buy a survival retreat that is way out in the country, which is what I recommend, then the chances are good that your property will be far away from the grid anyway. So much the better: if there truly is a zombie apocalypse, electrical lines will guide marauders to your house so that they can take over, and steal your food. A house with off-grid power does not have that issue.

But before I leave the issue of having power poles come to your property, there is one thing I want to mention: a lot of banks will not grant a construction loan for a house unless power poles at least come to the property. Many banks don't care if the electricity is actually used, only that the power poles extend into your property. It's like they have a fetish for power poles. So if you hope to someday get a bank loan to build a house, this is a consideration.

Now let me introduce you to the components of off-grid power systems.

As I wrote above, batteries and inverters are the heart of the system. But how many volts should your system be? The choices for a house system are 12, 24 and 48 volts. For a very simple system, like an RV, 12 volts will be fine. But for mid- to larger-sized houses, 24 to 48 volts systems are necessary. The more volts, the more expensive the battery banks.

If you are not sure of the size off-grid system you will need, you will need to figure the "electrical load" that your system will use. The websites that sell off-grid components often have "load calculators," where you can input how many people will live in your house, the appliances that they will use, and the wattage and voltage of your system will be figured out and given to you.

For 24 or 48 volt systems, there are several brands of batteries available, including Trojan, Hup, and Surrette. These batteries are extremely heavy –over 150 pounds or more -- and they sometimes have handy rope handles on them that would enable an Olympic weight-lifter to easily lift and move these batteries. For the rest of us, those rope handles would be considered nothing more than a cruel taunt. In the end, it is best to set up your battery area with the idea of moving these batteries around with a forklift.

You will also need to get copper cables to connect all these batteries. These cables eventually corrode near the batteries. And because of the high cost of copper nowadays, it is best to get cables that are a little longer than needed. That way, when the corrosion happens, instead of buying new cables you can just crimp them and install new battery connectors. (By the way, the high resale value of copper is one reason why thieves will want to trespass onto your property and steal this stuff, so you should guard and lock it up accordingly.)

Off-grid batteries typically last six to ten years before they will need to be replaced by another set of brand new batteries. For this reason, I think it is a good idea to set up space for *two* battery banks when you plan your off-grid power area. When you are ready to retire the old set of batteries and hook up the new set, all you would need to do is unhook the cable from the old batteries and re-attach it to the new batteries that are nearby. This will minimize the time your house will be without any power.

It is also important to keep your battery banks ventilated. Some people enclose their batteries inside waist-high walls of cinder-blocks, with a plywood top connected by hinges. The air around the batteries needs to be ventilated with outside air, but screens need to cover the outside hole of the ventilating pipe to keep mice from making themselves at home either in the pipes or near your batteries.

It is also a great idea to minimize the need for electricity in your house by replacing standard light bulbs with LED or fluorescent light bulbs, and by replacing electrical-powered appliances with those that use propane. There are some perfectly good propane-powered clothes dryers, refrigerators, freezers, water heaters, stoves and ovens for sale out there. Many of the websites that sell off-grid power components also sell these non-electrically powered appliances. Air conditioners also use a ton of electricity, so you should consider instead using a "swamp cooler," which is an evaporative-type cooler, for your house. Ceiling fans also make rooms feel cooler.

The placement and direction of the windows in your house can also have a huge influence on the warmth generated by the sun in your house. Of course, this would depend on where your house is located. A house in Arizona should probably have *no* windows that let in the sunlight, while a house in Alaska should have many windows letting in the sunlight and the sun's warmth.

And speaking of unconventional ways to cool your house, I have noticed many new houses and buildings are getting built with dirt and grass that covers some or all of the roof. Dirt weighs a lot, so I imagine that the load for this is huge. And it might be a little awkward to have to "mow the roof" from time to time. But hey, if you can do this, more power to you (pun intended).

Geothermal cooling is another way to cool a house with minimal electricity. The general idea of a geothermal system is to circulate fluid in buried hoses so that the constant 55-degrees of underground soil is harnessed and spread throughout the house by a fan that meets the hose as it brings cooled liquid up from the ground. Much of the cost associated with installing geothermal air conditioning systems comes from having to transport a backhoe to your property, and use it to dig the trenches where the hoses will be buried. For this reason, it might be a lot cheaper if you were to hire a geothermal AC contractor and allow them to use your backhoe (*see* Chapter 17).

An important component you will need in an off-grid power system is the charge controller. Batteries will last a lot longer when the power stored in them is constant, and this is the function of a charge controller. Inverters and charge controllers are sized according to your system. As brands go, people who know a lot more about off-grid power than I do tend to prefer the brands Xantex and Outback, with Outback getting a slight edge. These brands are also the most expensive.

There is also an off-grid power system component known as a "disconnect." A disconnect is basically a fuse box that enables you to connect and disconnect components of your systems without spikes in energy that could cause problems to parts of the system.

As for the power-generating parts of your system, while there are many options, solar panels (also called "photovoltaic" or PV) are getting cheaper and cheaper. Many years ago, I paid over $800 apiece for several 200-watt solar panels, and I bragged about the panels to anyone who was familiar with solar energy. Everyone was impressed, and they thought I was cool. Now you can buy 300-watt panels for less than $500 each.

There is now word yet on how long solar panels last, but it has to be a long time. I have heard of solar panels from the 1970's still powering houses out there.

I have always wondered about the possibility of hail damage, but solar panels nowadays are designed to withstand some pretty good hits of hail and still not break. High wind is a bigger issue, but that is more a function of sturdy connections between the solar panels and their racks. This issue should be taken seriously: as was shown in some recent hurricanes, an airborne solar panel can be a dangerous thing.

Wind turbines and hydroelectric power generators can also be used to power your batteries, but these have their own problems. Wind turbines may need to be repaired, and the bigger the turbine inside, the more complicated it is to put up and take down one of these things. Of course, for some people in the far north and south they might not have any choice but to use wind generators.

Micro-hydro systems are good, but only if there is a constantly-flowing river or stream nearby, and a government that is hands-off on water-diversion. See, the best micro-hydro systems divert part of the river or stream into a PVP pipe, which then runs a turbine wheel (similar to a car alternator), then dumps the water back into the river further downstream. Many local governments freak out at the prospect of a land-owner doing this, either totally forbidding it or allowing water diversion only after a lengthy, expensive and intrusive permit process.

Like I wrote above, the power level of your batteries will need to be at a constant level, and there will be times when the sun is weak, and the electricity demand in your house is high, so you will need a generator to occasionally charge the batteries. Most of the time, a generator that is rated at eight to twelve kilowatts will be fine.

Also, if you plan on doing any welding on your property, you will need at least an eight-kilowatt generator, and that is for very small welding jobs.

Another issue with generators is the danger of the exhaust. Carbon monoxide is deadly, and rarely can you tell when you are in the middle of it. If you do a YouTube
 search of the term "carbon monoxide," you will see many heart-breaking stories of people killed by generators running nearby. Campers, sailors, even people in a hotel were killed when a generator was running nearby, and the people unknowingly breathed carbon monoxide and never woke up.

For this reason, it is a good idea to keep your generator either out in the open, where you can be sure that the exhaust will safely vent, or if you want to minimize the generator's noise, in a separate shed, with the exhaust pipe connected with a duct pipe that goes out the structure. If you use a separate structure for your generator, you should have a lockable door on the structure, install a couple of carbon monoxide detectors inside of it, and post signs inside the structure that warn of the deadliness of carbon monoxide fumes.

Remember, people unfamiliar with your system, or even kids, might someday try to operate your system, and they might not be as paranoid of carbon monoxide fumes as you are.

As for brands of generators, Honda is my favorite brand, because they seem to really want to start and run smoothly, and they last a long time. But most of Honda generators are gasoline-powered, and they are pretty small in the amount of power they produce. Onan is also a good brand of generator. And I have been impressed with some Generac generators. There is also a very crude, old design of a diesel generator, named Lister, which reportedly runs forever.

The power source of your generator is another thing to consider. If you have a lot of propane appliances in your house, it might be worth it to also have a propane-powered generator.

Diesel might be a better power source for your generator, as diesel generators last a long, long time, and when you run out of diesel, you can run a diesel engine on filtered vegetable oil. Diesel generators also run on biofuel, which is complicated to make, but pretty cool.

Diesel fuel is usually cheaper to buy than propane, and you might be able to find even cheaper, "red" diesel, which is normal diesel fuel mixed with red coloring. They sell it that way so that non-highway vehicles like backhoes can buy it cheaper that diesel cars that run on the regular roads. If a diesel car is found with red diesel in the tank, the car owner gets a huge fine.

But whether you choose propane or diesel, large amounts of both can be delivered by local companies. Diesel is even delivered in its own barrel. (Of course, as with anyone coming onto your property, make sure that they are either trusted, or they think that someone is on your property all the time.)

I think that regular gasoline is way too dangerous to use for anything above a small, portable 2-kilowatt Honda generator. Gasoline fumes are very unstable and can cause a fire or even an explosion from the slightest spark, and you will need to store a lot of whatever power source you use for a generator. Gasoline also goes bad a lot faster than other energy sources.

But back to off-grid electrical components: if all this seems too complicated for you, check out off-the-shelf, complete systems that are offered by many of the sellers of off-grid energy systems. These businesses merely group together components that they think will work well together, and for the amount of electricity needed. Off-shelf systems may also have a slight savings because you are buying more components all at once from the same seller.

Another option available if you feel all this is too complicated: hire a consultant and pick his or her brain. I once hired author Jim Rawles for a one-hour consultation, and he was extremely informative. I also understand Scott Hunt offers a similar consultation. It is pricey – I paid Mr. Rawles $150 for one hour – but he answered all of the questions I had and more. He also allowed me to tape-record our conversation, so that I was able to re-listen to our talk later and let the terminology sink in better. Rawles is available through his website, survivalblog.com, and Scott Hunt is available through his website, practicalpreppers.com.

Here are some other websites I found where consultations are offered:
Offgridhardware.com (offer sales and consultations)
Buckvilleenergy.com (consulting)
Realgoods.com (consulting and classes)
Otherpower.com (sales, classes, books and consulting)
Earthhaven.org (consulting on a bunch of alternative fuel and other issues)

In my opinion, you should insist on tape recording any energy consultation that you pay for. You will be amazed at how fast new terms fly by, and you will not be able to take notes fast enough to properly understand all this as it is being explained to you.

Here are some sources for information and sales of the components of off-grid power systems: thesolarbiz.com, backwoodssolar.com, altenergymag.com, solarhomestead.com, and offthegridnews.com. Here are some other good websites for off-grid power components: theinverterstore.com, and wholesalesolar.com. Some of these websites have free "electronic load calculators" that will take your anticipated household energy use and calculate the size of off-grid system you will need.

For online purchases, check out jet.com, which is Walmart's new online store. Jet has some great prices on small off-grid energy systems.

Every once in a while, you can talk with someone at one of these websites who will talk with you on the phone directly and advise you on off-grid energy issues. For example, The Solar Biz has an engineer on staff, Tom, who spent a lot of time on the phone with me, and he answered many of my off-grid power questions.

I have also learned a lot about off-grid power from these YouTube channels: That Solar Guy, Tin Hat Ranch, Solar Power Videos, 7 Trumpets Prepper, TR Prepper, and Off Grid Build.

This is an incomplete list of websites that sell off-grid components or consulting services or YouTube channels. There is a lot out there, so do your own research.

Putting together an off-grid electrical system might seem complicated at first, but stay positive, and remind yourself that you can do it!

Chapter 24

Money-Making Ideas

Sometimes raw land gets a bad rap. A lot of people think of it as a money hole, which costs money and never makes any money for the owner. Not true!

Whether you want to have your retreat property help pay its mortgage payments, or you just want to have some extra money in your pocket, keep in mind that there is a lot you can do with raw land to make money. I present the ideas below as part of my goal of making your survival retreat as inexpensive as possible. Do your own research, and not all of these ideas will work, but here are enough ideas to get started. You can probably find more ideas online.

This one is probably the best way to make a lot of passive money with raw land: harvesting timber. If your property has a lot of forest on it (timber companies generally need at least 20 acres of forest), consider retaining a local forestry consultant to negotiate with timber companies to harvest the timber. Not only would you make money from the wood, but the timber companies will put in roads for their timber trucks. For some hilly properties, having someone start putting roads is a big deal. Of course, these roads will be dirt roads without any asphalt or gravel, but it is a great start.

It is possible to buy a huge piece of land (over 100 acres), and simultaneously negotiate the plans to harvest the timber and come out ahead financially. Way ahead.

If your property has a hill out in the country, consider negotiating with a local cell phone or Internet company to lease a hilltop for a signal tower. You might be able to negotiate free cell and wifi service for yourself and make some decent money. And the cell phone company may need to bring in some electrical lines for their tower. Bringing electricity to your property is usually a big expense.

On the other hand, if you have a lot of flat land on your property, you can lease grazing rights to ranchers. Not only do you make money from the rancher, but the animals also fertilize the land. It is all pretty hassle-free for the landowner: the cattle are dropped off, fed for a year or two, taken away to the slaughterhouse, then reappear at your local hamburger restaurant.

It is also possible to lease some or all of your land to hunters, for whatever period of times you wish. Check for the local hunting land lease agents in the area of your property. A liability insurance policy, which can be limited to the hunting leases and their durations, is also important.

If you have a lot of unused but fertile and mostly flat land, consider leasing the land to an orchard or vineyard company, or farm the land yourself. Every region has its most lucrative crops. For example, landowners in northern New York and Oregon are starting to grow a lot of grapes, while North Carolinians are now growing a lot of hops.

Your land might be in an area that would make it profitable to lease some of it to power companies to use for wind or solar power. Here is how it works: some group will put on the local ballot an initiative that will mandate that the power company generate a certain minimum amount of its power from "renewable" energy like solar or wind power. The power company urges a vote against it, citing the high cost, but it passes anyway.

Now, the power company looks for land to lease to have solar panels or wind turbines on. If you have ever driven east of Oakland, California, along Interstate 580, you have seen the wind turbines on mostly flat land, as far as the eye can see. That land was once considered too remote to do anything with until the landowner got together with the local energy company and worked out a deal.

Keep your eyes and ears open to minerals that could be harvested – by yourself or by a company doing the work – from your property. Depending on the region of the country where your property is, you could have below your land some oil or natural gas that could be brought up. Or you could lease to an energy company the "mineral rights" to your land.

Some parts of the country have land on which have been found gold. Think of the Sutter's Creek area of California in 1846: gold had never been found there before, and in fact, John Sutter was more interested in harvesting the timber there. Then he discovered some gold, and the rest is, as they say, history.

I wrote "keep your ears open" above because if you hear of a nearby property leasing mineral rights, or entering into an agreement with a gold mining company, maybe you could inquire about doing something similar for your land. Geology doesn't change on a dime, so any gold or other minerals found on a nearby piece of land could also be found on yours.

And finally, if your property is large enough, it is always possible to sub-divide part of it and donate it to the local government (maybe the park department) for a nice tax write-off. Admittedly, this sounds a lot simpler than it is, and this assumes the land has appreciated in value since you bought it.

You will first need to get the land surveyed and then legally subdivided. Then you will need to get an appraisal on the part of the land you want to donate, and you will need the local government to accept the land. But it is do-able and can help pay your taxes.

And speaking of sub-dividing, you never know if your property way out in the country may someday be surrounded by suburbia. Who knows? Intel might build a new plant, or Walmart might build a distribution center nearby. But if you find that your property that was once secluded in the middle of nowhere is now nearby a big need for housing, it would be worth looking into whether you can work with a real estate developer to subdivide the whole property and sell it to a new neighborhood of home-buyers. You will lose your secluded property out in the country, but with the profit you make from this, you can start all over again with another retreat property out in the country, somewhere else (*see* "Plan B For Bob Hope," in Chapter 1.)

Chapter 25

Your Retreat Team And Its Training

This issue is strictly a "personal choice" thing. When you have a survival retreat far away from the city, and a prolonged disaster hits the country, should you try to maintain and defend your retreat all by yourself and your family, or should you plan on having a survival retreat team with you? You may conclude, as have I, that it is simply not possible to do everything without help. That is why I recommend having a survival team in place, ready to go, in case of SHTF.

But whom should you invite to be part of the team? Confidentiality is important, so people cannot be casually invited before you get to know them. This narrows the list of possible team members to those you know well, either at the home area you decided to leave when you began the project to get a survival retreat or those neighbors who live nearby your survival retreat.

In my opinion, the ideal survival retreat team would include someone with intense medical experience, a farmer, a hunter, a mechanic, and a person who has a lot of knowledge maintaining and repairing guns. And maybe a ham radio operator. Throw in a few MacGyver types, who can take limited ingredients and make things work, and you could be set to go.

Notice that I used the term "ideal." You may find that the people you feel the most comfortable with in a zombie apocalypse are not the best-trained to do so. Or, you have come to admire someone with many important skills, but their personality is such that they won't get along with others and will be a detriment.

So your survival group does not have all the skills you wish you had. Start training. It is possible to train your group so that those important skills are honed so good that a group that started out as "almost as good" becomes prime.

And it can be fun, too. A survival group can set up evenings to have dinner together and watch a DVD on preparedness. After the DVD, it is important to set aside some time so that the group can discuss the issues presented in the DVD.

Here are a few online destinations to begin searching for DVDs that would help develop the survival skills of your group: Prepperacademy.com, disasterprep101.com, doomsdayprepperstraining.com, and preparednesspeace.com, which is my favorite small-group preparedness resource. Readygoprep.com also has some great group-preparedness resources. Some of these resources are expensive, so if nothing else, your group could just meet for dinner and watch a few group-preparedness YouTube videos afterward.

There is a pretty inexpensive resource out there, the Conflicted Card Game, found at conflictedthegame.com, for $20. Conflicted is not so much a card game as it is a chance for a group of people to discuss survival situations and choices that would have to be made in disaster situations. One example, chosen at random (and paraphrased), is this card: "You are on a business trip, 1,200 miles from home, when an EMP attack hits, frying all electronics and destroying the infrastructure. Store shelves will soon be bare, and food riots may not be far behind. You have $300 cash in your pocket. What would spend the money on and why, and how will you get home?"

There are also some great prepper conventions, like the Self-Reliance Expo and Prepper Camp, that are held several times a year. Oftentimes these conventions have workshops that are great for teaching the attendees valuable survival skills, not only for personal preparedness but also for family and group preparedness.

There is a great, and free, public resource available: CERT, or Community Emergency Response Teams, offered by FEMA. CERT classes are not so much in-depth prepping classes as they are classes to teach people to be more helpful, and less in the way when a disaster like a fire strikes a community. But the information in them is good. CERT classes can be found online at www.fema.gov/community-emergency-response-teams, and many CERT videotaped lectures can be found on YouTube.

The Red Cross offers all sorts of classes, including standard first aid, CPR, and EMT training. The classes are costly, with the charges for many classes going for $100 or more for an all-day class, but the information is good. You can find the classes offered by Red Cross at www.redcross.org/ux/take-a-class.

If you have ever been in a gun range with someone who has no experience handling a gun, you know the importance of gun safety training. The National Rifle Association lists many such courses, some online, at its website, which is https://firearmtraining.nra.org/.

I have not participated in them, but I have heard good things about Project Appleseed gun training events, which can be found at appleseedinfo.org.

If you arrange training for your group, the idea is to expand the knowledge of your group members in areas that they current know very little. For example, the gun expert in your group would probably benefit from training on emergency suturing, and if there is a nurse in your group, make sure he or she gets some gun safety training.

One last suggestion on survival group training, and admittedly this might seem out of left field, is to take a group member or two on a short-term mission trip. Not only will you help people in genuine need, but you will also learn valuable construction, farming, medical and sanitation skills. There are many mission groups out there, willing to take volunteers along for days or weeks at a time. Costs vary. Here are a few of them: groupmissiontrips.com, projects-abroad.org, ywam.org, water.cc, unitedplanet.org, experiencegla.com, and samaritanspurse.org.

Chapter 26

Easement And Squatting Issues

Okay, you have your survival retreat, and your fellow group-members are prepped and trained, and ready to survive the next zombie apocalypse. So far so good, right?

Not so fast, kemo sabe. City people don't know this as country people do, but you need to make sure your property is not being walked across or squatted on. That could lead to a loss of some or all of your property. Back when you lived on a quarter-acre in the city, watching for stuff like this was easy: you notice some of the grass on your front yard being thinned as the neighborhood forms a permanent trail there, or a neighbor moves a fence ten feet into your property. You can't help but notice encroachments like this. But what about a big piece of mostly undeveloped land, out in the country?

A brief primer on squatting, also known as adverse possession, and prescriptive easements is in order. The details vary in each state, but a prescriptive easement, which is a certain use that is taken away from the land owner, comes about when certain elements all line up at the same time. Those elements are: regular, uninterrupted, and open, non-permissive use of someone else's property, for five years or more.

If, for example, the neighborhood walked across part of someone's property for four years, then took a break for a year, then resumed the trail-walking for another couple years, then there is no prescriptive easement. If the neighborhood walked across someone's land for four years, and then the landowner began giving permission to everyone to do so, there is no prescriptive easement.

Squatting is similar, except instead of using someone else's property, the squatter just moves onto a property they don't own and lives there. Each state defines the period needed to live there before the squatter may legally take ownership of the property. Believe it or not, this still happens today. I recently found out that a woman with many parcels nearby my survival retreat acquired all those properties by squatting.

If you own a large piece of land and someone has set up a tent on a corner of it and lived there for many years, and you don't know about it, a court could order all or part of your land transferred to the person squatting there. Sometimes there are laws in different states that favor the land-owner, like the requirement that the squatter pays the property tax for the period of possession. But in general, the law imposes a duty on a landowner to periodically check his or her property and make sure that no one has moved onto it, or is using part of it. This is a kind of "you snooze, you lose" part of American property law.

Of course, there is one landowner that is protected above anyone else, and that is the government. So, if you have your sights set on that beautiful piece of land nearby that is owned by the government, think twice about trying to use it or move onto it and take it.

Owners of huge pieces of undeveloped property, say 100 acres or more, are really disadvantaged here. For land that big, it is nearly impossible to keep track of what is happening in all parts of the property. Google Earth could be helpful for a change, as you can log in and look at the furthest corners of your property and get a view of the land a year ago, or however long ago Google Earth photographed your land. Private drone services are also sprouting up, meaning that if there is such a service in your area, you could hire them to fly a drone over your property and videotape what's going on there. GoPro also sells a camera-equipped drone, called the "Karma," for $1,100 on Amazon, that you could buy and snoop on your own property.

If you find a trail across your property being worn from constant use, you should either fence it off to interrupt the use or post a sign granting permission. If you see someone living on part of your property, call the local sheriff to chase them off. I have even heard of groups of trespassers staking out a few acres at the back of a very inaccessible part of someone's land so that they can grow marijuana there. Most of the news made in such a situation involves whom should be prosecuted for cultivation, but the marijuana growers may also have a claim in civil court of adverse possession. It's possible!

Prescriptive easements and squatting might also be an issue with survival teams, where an owner allows survival team members to build sheds or dwellings on different parts of the owner's property. In such a situation, the landowner grants permission, so there is no squatting issue. But as with all legal issues, double-check to see what the rules are in your jurisdiction before letting someone spend a lot of time, or even letting them live on your land.

One disaster I could foresee is the situation where there is a falling out between the land-owner and a survival team member. If the landowner decides a certain team member should get lost, and tells them so, only to notice the team member still there five years later, then some or all of the landowner's property could be in jeopardy.

Proving use or possession is usually an issue with squatting or prescriptive easements. Take for example a case where a neighbor fences in some prime cattle grazing land that doesn't belong to him, and has his cattle graze there some or all of the year. When that neighbor goes to court and claims a prescriptive easement for grazing use of that property, he could present receipts and have testimony from the fence builder to prove the month and year that the pasture was enclosed with the fence. If the fence was built and the cattle grazing began over five years ago, then the absentee land-owner may have just lost the use of some of his property.

Prescriptive easements can cover all sorts of land uses. There is one case where a prescriptive easement was declared when a golf club had some golfers who were consistently bad so that they hit their golf balls onto a nearby property and then walked over the lot line and retrieved their golf balls. This went on for over five years, so the court declared that the golf club had a prescriptive easement on the neighboring properties, allowing the golfers to hit their golf ball onto the neighboring properties and then walk there and retrieve their golf balls.

Notice that many of these examples cited in this chapter are good for a chuckle or two, but the humor of it all vanishes when it is your property at stake. So, once you acquire a survival retreat, you should stay on top of it. Keep track of what is going on every square inch of your property, and defend your property rights!

Chapter 27

Trial Run: Spend The Night

There is something about having spent the night at your survival retreat. You just feel different about it.

When you feel that you have everything ready, set a night for you and your family to spend the night at your survival retreat. Don't be too ambitious this first time. A relatively cool, springtime, non-stormy night will do for this first night. But try your best to make everyone as comfortable there as they would be if they spent the night at home.

Right away, you will notice whether you have the ability to make a good dinner for your family. A campfire or a propane-powered camping stove would enable this. Were there enough napkins and utensils to enable everyone to eat what you served them? The Moroccan-style of eating food with your hands works well in Morocco, but not at a survival retreat in the United States. How about chairs and a table for the meal? Make sure all this is covered, and if not, put it on the list for next time. In fact, you may find that you will need to make a long list of corrections to make for next time.

After dinner, is everyone able to brush their teeth and wash their faces in clean water, before heading to bed? These are nighttime routines that will keep everyone comfortable. Make a note of whatever needs improving next time.

When everyone goes to bed, are they all warm, comfortable and safe from mosquitos and animals where they are sleeping? If not, add the required adjustments to your list.

During the night, was everyone able to get to the restroom if needed? Was there enough light in the form of lanterns and flashlights to enable family members to get around in the dark? This could lead to more additions to your list.

In the morning, were you able to make a good breakfast for everyone?

Did you have a trash bag ready to collect all the trash that everyone generated? That is one I always missed, early on. I guess it's because trash bags may be the least-exciting items to pack on an overnight trip.

Trash bags will work for plastic utensils and paper plates, but if you used metal utensils and permanent plates, you would need to arrange for some kind of basin to hold water, and dishwashing soap and towels to dry them.

Some parts of the event may be uncomfortable, but try your best to be as upbeat as possible. Think of this as a new adventure for you and your family. On the drive home, ask everyone for suggestions on what improvements should be made for next time.

You may notice, as did I, that you feel differently about your survival retreat now, and you know what is needed to make the place more livable.

.

Chapter 28

Odds And Ends

In this chapter, I will discuss a few final issues.

Flashlights And Batteries

If you have lived most of your life in a city, you will probably not have a good idea of what it is like to be in total darkness. In the city, at night, if the moon is not out, there is always a street light or a car nearby with its headlights on.

When I moved to the country, I was surprised at how totally dark things could get at night. I mean, *really* dark! Not only is nighttime light a safety issue against intruders on your survival retreat, but it is also an issue with dangerous animals that come out at night and hunt for food. A flash of a strong light into a nighttime woodland can often reveal the reflection of the retinas of animals looking back at you. Whether it is a raccoon or a mountain lion, an animal that has just had its eyes flashed with a bright flashlight will be slightly blinded, and they will stay away from you.

It is for that reason that it is important to have some good flashlights and rechargeable batteries, and solar battery chargers with you at your survival retreat.

I have several Goal Zero solar battery chargers. At $100 apiece, they put a dent in my budget, but they are pretty durable and do the job. C. Crane makes a more affordable charger at $25, but I think it feels cheap. SunJack makes an affordable solar battery charger, which sells for $15, and will hook into a solar panel that has a USB port. (If you have AC power available, I have always been very impressed with the La Crosse and Powerex brands of battery chargers.)

For flashlights and batteries, numbers are important and will lead you to the products you should buy. You need flashlights with a high number of "lumens," which is the international standard of light. Lumens are usually listed on flashlights for sale, and it is not uncommon to find flashlights with LED lightbulbs that can emit 100 or more lumens. I recently found a great J5 mini-flashlight that emits 400 lumens, priced at $19 on Amazon. I also have several waterproof Dorcy flashlights, which emit 150 lumens and cost only $8 on Amazon.

Flashlights made to wear on your head have not been perfected yet. This is a need that often arises when I have to carry something around in the dark. However, the J5 flashlight mentioned above, and occasionally others, come with a belt clip that can be clipped onto the bill of a baseball cap.

I also like the dual-use quality of Maglite flashlights, which can also be used as a baton for self-defense. Police departments have these. But the lumens emitted for the various Maglite models top out at 150, with most of the Maglites rated as having less than 100 lumens.

Another problem with Maglite flashlights is that a lot of their models use C or D-sized batteries, while I like to keep only AA and AAA-sized rechargeable batteries. As for brands of rechargeable batteries, the numbers for milliamp hours and number of possible rechargings are best with Eneloop and Eneloop Pro batteries.

I would caution against buying items, like flashlights, which have an internal battery and a hand-crank charger. Usually, these items are sold without any specifications on the power storage abilities of the rechargeable battery inside, and the battery wears out pretty fast.

One last thing about batteries: if all you have are alkaline batteries, when they corrode the flashlights or whatever you have them inside, don't throw away the corroded item. You can use q-tips with vinegar or baking soda and water to clean the corrosion off.

In time, you will find that you will have a lot of items that use batteries that will need to be changed from time to time. For this reason, I recommend putting a small piece of masking tape on the outside of each item that has batteries inside it and writing on the masking tape the date you put the batteries in. This will help you gauge when you need to replace the batteries.

Old Clothes, Blankets, And Used Sleeping Bags

In my last book on prepping, *Dirt Cheap Valuable Prepping*, I made a big deal about the news reports of homeless people in the winter, and how tragic it was that they were so cold and lacked warm clothes. Then it hit me, as I hope it hit the reader, that in a societal collapse situation, we will all be homeless. And as people who could be homeless, we should take precautions.

I'm talking about old clothes, including coats, and blankets. But instead of going to Amazon or a physical store and buying all this stuff brand new, we should go and instead buy this stuff at Goodwill or Salvation Army thrift stores. I still think that is a great idea. Don't worry about what the coats or blankets will look like – if it keeps you warm in the winter, it serves its purpose.

Sleeping bags are a special case. I'll never forget walking through an REI store and pricing their sleeping bags. $200 on up! And when it comes to sleeping bags that keep you warm, other stores and almost as pricey.

But instead of buying a sleeping bag from a store, go to EBay and shop for a used sleeping bag. You will be amazed at the low cost charged for some very high-end sleeping bags on EBay. It's like the market for used sleeping bags is somehow skewed. Maybe potential buyers don't want to buy a sleeping bag that other people have already slept in. If you feel that way, buy one used and spend some money getting it dry cleaned before you use it. There is simply no reason not to buy a high-quality, used sleeping bag on EBay.

Night Vision

Let's face it: seeing clearly at night is one of those things that is very important in a societal collapse. In case of SHTF, you and your survival team meet at your survival retreat, where you could be besieged by others trying to get your stuff, or by animals who are out for the night, looking for something or someone to eat. Night vision is very important.

The problem is that until recently, the only decent night vision monoculars cost $4,000 on up. Enter the new FLIR Scout TK pocket-sized night vision monocular, which costs around $500 on Amazon. This thing is amazing! The clarity of what you can see at night, even things at 300 yards, will surprise you. The one drawback to this monocular is the internal battery, which must be charged up. Hopefully, the folks at FLIR will someday power this thing with AA batteries that can be replaced as needed.

Even more impressive, mostly because of its price, is the Solomark Night Vision Monocular, which goes for around $140 on Amazon. While not perfect, this is a good night vision monocular that enables you to adjust the infra-red level and zoom, and take videos and photos, which you can then upload to your computer. I also like the fact that this unit is powered by AA batteries.

In the future, there will no doubt be other entrants into the field of night vision, and prices will continue to fall. So you should keep watching this sector. Someday the nighttime vision quality of the FLIR piece above will be paired with the versatility and method of power of a Solomark, for even less money.

Beware Of Friends Bearing Junk

Earlier in this book, I discussed the hazard of thieves coming onto your survival retreat and taking your stuff away, and ways that you can deter or stop them.

But what happens if the opposite happens? What happens if you become friends with a group of locals, say a church or civic group or just people living nearby, and they begin to volunteer all sorts of things that they feel you need to have at your property? You know, "just in case." In a short amount of time, you can find that part of your land has become a receptacle for junk that you will probably never need, and it starts to look pretty ugly.

This is one of those embarrassing moments, but I hope you learn from my experience. After I had my property for a few years and I had gotten to be friends with some of the neighbors, I began noticing that they would sporadically arrive and bring with them something that they were sure I would need someday. One neighbor gave me an old kitchen cabinet. Someone else gave me a half-empty can of light green, interior paint. Another neighbor generously donated his favorite hubcap. And yet another neighbor gave me a broken 500-watt generator, which he swore would work someday after it got some TLC. My property is pretty big, so at first, I didn't think much of it. But before long, a part of my property started looking like a trash dump, and I have since been removing items and taking them to a nearby landfill.

Sure, it is awkward when I later encounter the donators of this stuff and explain to them that I never found a need for their donated items and had to get rid of them. But it is also a waste of my time in removing and disposing of those items. And this is time that I would rather spend preparing my survival retreat.

So, be on your guard: not only is there a danger in people coming to your property to take things away from you, but there is also a danger in friends coming onto your property, bearing junk that they want to give you. As they are friends and neighbors – let's face it, they mean well -- you shouldn't be rude, but be ready with friendly but firm reasons why you doubt you would ever need that item. One thing that worked for me once was a suggestion to the donator that they keep that item on *their* property so that I know where I can find it if I ever need it.

Junk Land Chapter From DCVP

Before this book, I published a book entitled *Dirt Cheap Valuable Prepping: Cheap Stuff You Can Stockpile Now That Will Be Extremely Valuable When SHTF*. I use the initials "DCVP" when I refer to that book.

If I may say so, DCVP is chock-full of good ideas for prepping. It is not meant to be the first or the main prepping book you have, like a book that would explain the prepping basics, but it is meant to be the second or third book that should be included in every prepper's library. I like to think that the DCVP book has a "twist" on many of the main issues of prepping. One example is that in that book I discourage the reader from stocking up on single-use toilet paper that could be devoured by rats where it is stored, but instead to buy a few travel bidets, which are durable and can be reused.

Below is a reprint of the "Junk Land" chapter from DCVP. Many of the issues in that chapter are covered in this book, but you might find it helpful nevertheless. Enjoy!

Junk Land

A lot of preppers have the idea that it is good to stockpile "junk silver," dimes and quarters that are minted before 1965, and they are right. If the end comes, these coins will be something you can have on hand to buy stuff you need.

But I would like to encourage you to buy "junk land," which is raw land that is cheap and plentiful, and out in the country. Realtors call it "raw land" because it is a parcel of land and nothing is there, not even roads, electricity or water. Many times the owner has inherited this land, or a larger parcel has been divided and parts of it are put up for sale. Despite the number of acres that make up the size of the property, the land is sometimes hard to sell, and the owner will offer to finance the purchase for you.

Raw land is a prepper's dream! If the sewage really hit the fan, where else can you go to survive but in the country? And with several acres under your control, you can plant food, forage for food, store some supplies, hunt, live, and survive.

The way you find this raw land is to locate an area outside of a suburban area, sometimes 100 or more miles away, and do a Google search for the terms "raw land" "acreage" and "owner finance." You will be amazed at the numbers of acres available for sale at relatively low prices.

It will be a different experience for people who were born and raised in cities. People who have spent most of their lives in cities will figure that 50 – 100 acres of land will cost millions of dollars. And they are right, so long at the land is surrounded by neighborhoods and roads! But if you look closely, you can find this much land for sale, for low prices, out in the country.

Part of the reason for the low prices on acreage in the country is because the land is pretty inaccessible to where people want to live and work. So much the better! To survive a true SHFT situation, you want to have land that is far away from where people live and work; far away from interstate highways. This is truly unglamorous, tucked-away, mostly inaccessible land that no one wants. When hordes of people march out of the cities to look for food and farms to take over, they will mostly stick to the interstate highways, and the further your property is from one of these, the better.

Here are some priorities I suggest in your search for junk land: make sure it is a big piece of land, preferably 20 acres or more. With 20 acres or more, you may be able to go truly unnoticed by the neighbors or travelers nearby. Being unnoticed is very important.

Once you buy the land, explore it. Bring some saws and pruning shears and cut a hiking trail into the middle of your property. If your land is hilly, find a flat area. In time, your hiking trail will become worn, and someday you can hire a local bulldozer operator to come onto your land and turn your hiking trail into a small road that you can drive on. Make sure there are some "turn around" areas adjacent to the road, and you will need to hire local people to come to your property and spread some gravel so that you don't get stuck or slide off the road when it rains.

The thing to keep in mind about gravel is that once it is spread out on your roads, you need to drive on it after it gets wet and then apply another layer of gravel. And after it rains again, maybe a third layer of gravel! Eventually, the gravel will be packed in tight, and the road will be just as secure as if it were paved. Also, make sure that you have some water ditches on each side of the roads so that your roads do not get washed away in a heavy rainstorm.

Water is also very important. Ideally, the land would have a running stream, but if that is not available, consider having a water well drilled uphill from any possible building site. Ask the neighbors how successful they have been in drilling wells that produce water. Usually, parcels of land that are near each other will have similar water well issues.

I had some success in hiring a "douser," or a "water witch," to come to our property and find areas that would be good bets to dig a well. A person who does this work does not engage in witchcraft but instead measures changes in magnetic attractions from one step on your property to another. If the magnetism changes abruptly, the person figures that this is an area that would be good to dig a water well.

It worked on our property. We hired a water well driller to dig a water well (costing us about $9,000) at one of the locations the douser had selected. The well-driller dug down about 200 feet, and our well was tested to produce seven gallons of water per minute. The well-driller "cased" the hole with PVC pipe and we hired someone else to put in a hand-powered water well pump, and that cost less than $1,000. At some point in the future, we will address the "hardness" of the water, which is a measure of various minerals in the water, but the water is still drinkable.

One issue in buying raw land is that the land should, if affordable, be surveyed so that you know where the boundaries of the land are. This can be pretty expensive, especially with larger parcels of land whose boundaries will go through dense forest. If the survey job costs way too much money, it still might be possible to compare notes with the neighbor on the approximate land boundaries.

Another issue with buying raw land in the country is that many times the land in question is land-locked. That might be why that 100 acres lot, for example, only a few miles outside of a small town, with beautiful rolling hills, in so cheap. I have heard horror stories of people buying property out in the country, which is beautiful and just a short hike through the neighbor's land. Eventually, "no trespassing" sign go up, lawyers' letters are mailed telling the land-locked land owner to stay off of the land between a road and the destination property, and the land-locked land truly becomes inaccessible and worthless. A face-to-face meeting with the neighbor results in no permission to get to the land-locked land, and the phrase "you should have thought about this when you bought the land" is spoken. Truly a nightmare!

However, a good prepper should view land-locked land as an opportunity, not a setback. Ultimately, your goal will be to buy a permanent "easement road" from your neighbor so that you can drive from a local road, through your neighbor's property, to your land so that it is no longer land-locked. This can be tricky, but it is doable. The extra hassle in getting an easement road explains the lower price of land-locked properties.

Before buying some land-locked land, you will need to approach the neighbor who owns the land between the land-locked property and the road and ask to buy an option to purchase an easement road through their land. Of course, an offer for money will be involved, and the land-owner may know that they have you at a disadvantage. But sometimes the neighbor will have a contracting or construction company that you can offer to hire to work on the road once you own the land and have the easement. Or there might be some other enticements you can offer.

In some jurisdictions, you can offer to trade some land with the neighbor, and this is called a "lot line adjustment," so that you could own a stretch of land between the land-locked property and a nearby road, and your neighbor will get the same area of the land-locked property in exchange. This solution to a land-locked property might be something that no one has ever thought of.

In either case, an option to buy an easement, or an option to do a lot-line adjustment, you must have this in hand before you buy the land-locked property. If you don't have this taken care of before you buy the land, it could be too late. The owner of the land between your property and the road will know that he or she has a serious upper hand with you.

The details of getting an option to buy an easement, and the legalities of it all are outside the scope of this book, and I am not here to give you real estate legal advice. But just keep in mind that it is possible to turn a land-locked property into an accessible property, and doing so may only be a hurdle or two away. Educate yourself on the local easement laws, find a local real estate attorney and tell him or her your goals, and go for it. It is possible that you could buy some land that really is valuable but no one else wanted because of the accessibility issues. But be careful.

Once you own the land, familiarize yourself with the local county rules for developing, building roads, drilling wells, building structures, and leaving vehicles there. In talking with county officials, your attitude should be "I want to comply with the rules," but it is a good idea to keep your specific plans to yourself. I remember once speaking with someone at my county's building permit office, and I asked about some rules about building a structure smaller than is required to get a permit. "Hey, be careful what you do," he sneered at me. "If we find out where your property is and that you have built something against the rules without a permit, you will have repercussions." I answered, "That's is why I am here asking you what the rules are."

You should also keep track of your property, and you should fence off your property so that hikers don't wander onto your property and get injured and sue you. Also – and I have never seen this, but I have heard of it – a property that has no fences could find itself explored by local county officials, looking for code violations.

Any workers you hire to come to the property and do work should be scrutinized. They will probably realize that this is a property that is vacant most of the time, so they could always come back later, when you aren't there, and help themselves to whatever is there. I had a couple of generators stolen, and I strongly suspect a couple of the workers I hired to come by to do some work. Since then I have built sheds that are burglar-proof, and I keep my generators and tools there.

As you get more experienced with your property, you will find that you have all sorts of things that are left there, and they are liable to the stolen if they are not secured. Costco sells a pretty cheap shed that can be locked. In some areas, a small wooden shed can be bought and the seller will construct it for you at the area you choose.

Possibly the best and cheapest structure you can put on your property is either a used RV or a school bus. I have been amazed at how cheap old RV's and school buses are on EBay. Either one could be bought for very little money, and parked in an area that is not easily seen outside the property. Then the RV or school bus should be painted dark green or tan camouflage, depending on the terrain. Then it could the locked to secure your tools and other valuables, and you will have a quick and easy place to stay once you get onto your property.

A front gate is also important, and there is a company called Mighty Mule that sells battery-operated front gate openers that can be installed and powered by solar panels. They work great, and they are available at Tractor Supply stores. In some jurisdictions, you must post "no trespassing" signs before you can get the police to prosecute anyone found trespassing on your property.

But it all starts with finding raw land at a price that you can afford. Below are some websites that I have found that list raw land for sale, and sometimes the properties are offered with owner financing.

You can check out the website Survival Realty for some ideas, but keep in mind these houses are mostly for millionaire preppers who don't mind if their prepper location has already been publicized everywhere. In my opinion, this is just not very realistic. But the website is still interesting and generates ideas of what a good if overdone prepper location is like.

There are many others, but here are some other websites that list raw land, some of which are offered with owner financing:

Countryplacesinc.com – Tennessee, Alabama and Kentucky
Billyland.com – western USA
Inlandproperties.com – northern SF Bay Area
Hillcountryrealestate.net – TX Hill Country
Landsofmissouri.com – Missouri
Floridaland1.com – central Florida land

Dealing With Lawyers

Through the years, I have had friends who have had legal matters that, for whatever reason, I have not handled for them. In many of those cases, I have given my advice to my friends on how they should go about contacting, retaining and dealing with the attorney who will eventually handle some legal matter. I thought I would do that here with you.

And this assumes your questions are not answered by cheaper means, like reading a self-help legal book, some of which I list in the Additional Resources part of this book. And you never know, Chapter 2, with its discussion of easement roads and accessibility, may not be the only issue that comes up that would require you to ask for the services of an attorney. You might have other property issues that necessitate the hiring of an attorney.

Although I am an attorney, you should not consider me your attorney, and for that matter, I am not giving you specific legal advice. But here are a few of my thoughts:

First off, keep in mind what you may be hiring an attorney to do: advising you on the legal issues you are wading through, and drafting the legal documents that you will eventually file with the local county property office, to formally make your property transactions legitimate. The chances of going to a trial on anything are pretty low. That means that you will most likely be looking for a book-smart attorney, not an outwardly aggressive and/or flamboyant courtroom attorney.

Where to find an attorney is another consideration. Many counties have a bar association that has a lawyer referral service. You can find the phone number by Googling it or by looking in the local Yellow Pages. In your initial phone calls, if you are calling about a sensitive matter, I would be vague about why you are calling. It is okay to say that you wish to inquire about legal services relating to an easement or a purchase of property, or whatever your legal need is. *Only* your conversations with an actual attorney or the attorney's employees are privileged and confidential.

Many, but not all, states allow you to look up on the state bar website whether an attorney you are considering has had any disciplinary proceedings against him or her. Start by Googling your state's "state bar," and when you get to that website, you can look up the attorney. The information posted will usually include the attorney's address, phone number, e-mail address, law school information, and any legal specialties. Somewhere on the page, there could be a link for any disciplinary proceedings that have been filed against the attorney. An example would be that the attorney was once charged with having an alcohol problem that affected his or her work. Most attorneys have no record of any disciplinary proceedings whatsoever, but it might be worth checking out, just in case.

It also might be worth it to look up your prospective attorney on Twitter, Instagram, and Facebook. You never know what you might find out about them there, and it is a totally public record.

Cost: Before you hire any attorney, you should call and discuss your legal issues and possible fees with at least three local attorneys. Ask their fee schedules and what other else you will be billed for. Sometimes attorneys will charge for making Xerox copies, and I have always wondered whether it takes more time for the attorney to bill for the copy than it takes even to make one.

Also, ask whether the attorney is open to cost-cutting ideas. As an example, in the case of my property, the easement road was basically an "S" shaped road, and I walked to the area of the proposed easement road with a GPS monitor, and wrote down in the easement document the coordinates of the road, its connection to the public road, its main turns, and then the road's connection with my property. I saved a lot of money doing it that way. An overly-cautious attorney might have insisted that a formal survey be done on my proposed easement road, and that would have cost me many thousands of dollars in surveyor fees.

Regarding expertise: ask whether the attorney has ever done the specific task that you need him or her to do. If not, you could find that you have been billed to educate the attorney for your issue.

In dealing with your attorney, stay cheerful and respectful. Make sure to laugh at any jokes or humorous stories the attorney tells you. Alright, that might have been a bit much, but you get the idea. Keep in mind that not every attorney has to take as a client anyone who calls him or her. You could be turned down as a client!

See, in your initial conversations with the attorney, *you* are also making a pitch to the attorney that you will be a good client. And a good client not only means that you will pay your legal fees on time, but also that you will be pleasant to work with. You want your attorney to enjoy dealing with you, and quickly returning your phone calls or e-mails.

You can admit to the attorney that your knowledge of legal terms is limited and that you would like to keep as much of your communications written down, in the form of letters and e-mails, so that you can re-read the correspondence later and follow along what is happening. You might be surprised at how you will have the same legal questions, again and again, only to find out that the issue was already discussed in an e-mail a few weeks earlier.

Some attorneys might feel awkward about this one, but if you are brave, you can request to tape record your phone conversations with your attorney. A paranoid attorney might be worried that you will later spring the recording of a previous phone call and ask to explain an apparent contradiction with a later comment. But here is where I am coming from on this: it has amazed me at how many times I have answered and re-answered the same legal questions from my clients. I understand that this is a new world of thinking for my client. But for me, the legal issues are pretty routine. In the few times I have had a client ask to tape record a conversation with me, I readily agree, because I know that this client will not ask the same legal questions every few weeks.

But, as I wrote, not many attorneys would agree to let you tape record a phone conversation with them. And, by the way, *always* ask beforehand for the consent of *anyone* whose phone conversation you wish to record, whether the phone conversation will be with an attorney or with a normal person.

E-mail exchanges are great for the same reason. New ideas and issues can be discussed in a format that you can keep and re-read later. Keep the e-mails with your attorney short. You can ask the attorney a couple of specific legal questions, and you should make sure to keep the return e-mails, or even print them out. That way, you can read and re-read them, and you will eventually understand the legal issues discussed.

Before engaging in later phone calls or e-mails, make sure to listen to or read all or at least most previous correspondences with the attorney. You would hate to pay for the same legal advice a second or third time.

When you get your monthly fee statement, I would advise that you look it over and make sure that whatever communications you are billed for actually happened. It is rare, but it is possible that billing records can get mixed up. If you have a dispute, you should make sure that your concerns are expressed, but keep the attitude that if certain work was actually done for you, then you owe that legal fee.

It is perfectly appropriate to restrict the work your attorney will do for you, and you can even ask your attorney *not* to work on certain issues, or to handle certain correspondence. Sometimes you can handle your own legal correspondence, or file your legal documents with the county. Paying an attorney to do certain menial things only costs money unnecessarily.

But throughout your relationship with your attorney, keep things professional and respectful. With the right attitude and the correct approach, you will probably find that you have gotten a lot of value from your relationship with your attorney.

Dealing With Contractors

For small and big jobs that you want to have someone else do, you will have to hire a local contractor. I have to admit that almost all of my experiences with contractors have been positive, but I thought I would include a few bits of advice here on dealing with contractors.

Keep in mind that all a contractor has to do to be a contractor is to post a bond, and, in most states, pass a state contractor's exam. A lifetime of doing carpentry work, or in being an honest person with a great reputation are not requirements to being granted a contractor's license. I have found some with those qualities, but still…

In my opinion, there are two important factors to consider in whom to hire as your contractor: how long they have been in business, and any recommendations you can get from their former clients.

You can look up some of your contractor's history at the website of your state's contractor licensing board. As you might expect, all states are different, but most will show you whether the contractor's license is current, and a history of the bonds posted by the contractor, disciplinary history, and sometimes the workman's compensation history. Not all of the information posted is that important, but you can check it all out and see the earliest year this contractor posted a bond, and whether there have been any times that the contractor was not bonded. This could mean that for a while the contractor worked for someone else, or spent a year or two in rehab.

More so than with attorneys, it also might be worth looking up your prospective contractor on social media, like Twitter, Instagram, and Facebook. People always seem to post the most intimate details of their lives on social media. A few years ago, I had a client who was a chef, and he claimed he was "seriously addressing" the alcohol problem that got him into trouble. A day after St Patrick's Day, I checked out his Facebook page and saw that he had posted a video of himself and a friend repeatedly pounding down tequila shots. Thanks for the clarification!

I have not had any luck with the online rating services, like Angie's List, Better Business Bureau, Consumers' Checkbook, and Yelp, but it might be worth checking them out to see if they have background on a contractor you are considering.

Contractors don't like being watched while they work, but you should periodically check in on their progress anyway. If there are mistakes in an approach to a certain job, it is best to catch the mistake early while it is still relatively cheap to fix it.

If a contractor is consistently late on the completion of his or her jobs, or the work is more often than not bad work, then it would be a good idea to let the contractor go and find another one to work with. No angry speech is necessary; just a comment along the lines of "let's face it; this isn't working out…" The contractor will probably have other clients, whose needs are more compatible with his or her abilities.

In dealing with contractors, remember that you are entering into a contract, and either a written agreement on paper or e-mail is good to have so that both sides can refer to what was agreed to. Of course, not everything during an on-going job can be written down and agreed to, which brings us back to whether you trust the contractor.

Additional Resources

There aren't many books out there that discuss getting a survival retreat and how to inexpensively fortify it once you have it. *Dirt-Cheap Survival Retreat: One Man's Solution*, by M.D. Creekmore, is an exception. I was very impressed with that book.

I was also impressed with the details of off-grid power that was listed in the book *Going Off The Grid: The How-To Book Of Simple Living And Happiness*, by Gary Collins. As I wrote in Chapter 23 of this book, off-grid power is very complicated, and Collins explains it well.

The Complete Battery Book, by Richard Perez, is very helpful in figuring out off-grid power systems.

Off Grid Solar, by Joseph O'Connor, is another good book on off-grid power systems.

On the subject of your survival retreat team, Charley Hogwood has two excellent books out there: *The Survival Group Handbook: How To Plan, Organize, And Lead People For A Short Or Long Term Survival Situation*, and *MAGS: The People Part of Prepping: How To Plan, Build, and Organize a Mutual Assistance Group in a Survival Situation*. Hogwood also has a great website, readygoprep.com, with all his books and some helpful DVD's. I have heard that he offers consulting services.

I have hired James Wesley Rawles for consultation, and I was very happy with it. Rawles can be hired for consultation by contacting his assistant at Survivalblog.com, which is one of the best prepper websites out there.

Rawles has also written some very helpful books: *Patriots*, *How To Survive The End Of The World As We Know It*, and *Tools For Survival*, all of which should be a part of everyone's prepper library.

Here are some additional resources regarding the legal issue discussed in this book:

When it comes to self-help legal books, I have always been impressed with the books from Nolo Press. These books are written by attorneys on most every legal issue you might encounter, and the books are written with a minimum of legalese. In other words, the books by Nolo are written so that non-attorneys can understand the legal issues they are encountering.

Specific to real estate issues, Nolo has a great book with an edition that has just recently been published: *Neighbor Law: Fences, Trees, Boundaries & Noise, 9th Edition*, by Attorneys Emily Doskow and Lina Guillen. This is an excellent all-around real estate law book, and it covers the legal issues discussed in this book.

Also, the Nolo Press website, nolo.com, has a legal question-and-answer section, located at nolo.com/lawyers, in which you can consult with or ask an attorney in your state specific legal questions. Any follow-up, or even retaining the attorney, is up to you.

Nolo's *Encyclopedia of Everyday Law: Answers to Your Most Frequently Asked Legal Questions, 10th Edition*, by Attorney Shae Irving, is a good book on basic legal principles. While I fund this book to be very cursory on the issues discussed in this book, Irving's book is filled with good, basic summaries of most legal issues you will face in life, including real estate issues. This is a book you could buy and just put on your bookshelf, to use anytime most any legal issue comes up in your life.

Neighbors From Hell (NFH): Managing Today's Brand of Conflict Close to Home, by Bob Borzotta, is a book that does not exactly cover the legal issues discussed in this book, except for (briefly) shared driveways and adverse possession. But when I read NFH, I was impressed at how the book at least offers a basic education in real estate law.

Acknowledgments

I wish to acknowledge the following people from whom I have gotten some good ideas or had various questions answered:

David Kobler, also known as Southerprepper1, whose books and YouTube videos on prepping have been excellent and thought-provoking. In my phone calls and e-mail exchanges with Kobler, I have found that he is very helpful and pleasant to deal with.

James Wesley Rawles, who has written some very helpful books. His books, *Patriots*, *How To Survive The End Of The World As We Know It*, and *Tools For Survival*, should be a part of every prepper's library. You can hire Rawles for phone consultations by e-mailing his assistant at his website. Rawles' website, Survivalblog.com, is one of the best prepper websites out there.

Scott Hunt, who authored *The Practical Preppers Complete Guide to Disaster Preparedness*. I find that I keep referring to this book. On YouTube, Hunt is known as Engineer 775, and his how-to videos are excellent.

The author Angery American, who is himself an electrician, was helpful answering my questions on off-grid power.

MD Creekmore, who authored *Dirt-Cheap Survival Retreat: One Man's Solution*. Also, check out Creekmore's other books, *31 Days to Survival*, *The Prepared Prepper's Cookbook*, and *The Prepper's Guide to Surviving the End of the World As We Know It*, and his website, TheSurvivalistBlog.net.

So far without exception, the world of prepper authors, podcasters, and YouTube video producers have been very helpful to me. I have found that this group is very open to being contacted with questions.

My online friends have also been a big help with this book. Thanks to those who have contacted me and have offered to write testimonials about various survival retreat issues. I like to include these in my books because they seem to break things up and make my book more readable.

I also wish to thank my many friends, family members and beta readers who continually offered constructive criticism on the on-going writing and revisions on various drafts of this book. Thanks especially to my wife, who was always available at any time, for readings and suggested corrections of this book.

Cal Wilson
May, 2017

www.ingramcontent.com/pod-product-compliance
Lightning Source LLC
Chambersburg PA
CBHW062006280526
45787CB00005B/1998